Galina Kozhevnikova

in collaboration with Alexander Verkhovsky and Eugene Veklerov

ULTRA-NATIONALISM AND HATE CRIMES IN CONTEMPORARY RUSSIA

The 2004-2006 Annual Reports of Moscow's SOVA Center

With a foreword by Stephen D. Shenfield

ibidem-Verlag
Stuttgart

Bibliografische Information der Deutschen Nationalbibliothek
Die Deutsche Nationalbibliothek verzeichnet diese Publikation in der
Deutschen Nationalbibliografie; detaillierte bibliografische Daten sind im
Internet über http://dnb.d-nb.de abrufbar.

Bibliographic information published by the Deutsche Nationalbibliothek
Die Deutsche Nationalbibliothek lists this publication in the Deutsche Nationalbibliografie;
detailed bibliographic data are available in the Internet at http://dnb.d-nb.de.

Coverpicture: DPNI activists on a Russian march, Moscow, 2007 (DPNI stands for *Dvizhenie protiv nelegal'noy immigratsii* - Movement Against Illegal Immigration). Photograph by © Alexander Verkhovsky, 2007.

∞

Gedruckt auf alterungsbeständigem, säurefreiem Papier
Printed on acid-free paper

ISSN: 1614-3515

ISBN-10: 3-89821-868-6
ISBN-13: 978-3-89821-868-9

© *ibidem*-Verlag
Stuttgart 2008

Printed in Germany

Contents

II. The 2005 Annual Report

III. The 2006 Annual Report

6

7

List of Tables

Foreword

The continuing salience of various kinds of violent racism, radical nationalism, and even fascism in Russian political life is naturally a matter of concern and anxiety for very many people both in Russia itself and in other countries. But just how significant are these phenomena? Are they still growing, or have they perhaps now reached their peak? How effectively are Russian society and the Russian state meeting the challenge? What difference has Putin's accession to power made?

Western and Russian observers have expressed sharply divergent opinions on these and other pertinent questions. Not all opinions, however, are of equal value. Some are based on the best available information and analysis. Others reflect undeclared biases and unverified assumptions, or at best impressions gained from experience of limited scope (in terms of geography, for instance). Unfortunately, opinions expressed by academics do not always come under the former category.

The foreigner who wishes to form opinions in this area but who does not have a fluent reading knowledge of Russian has a special handicap. The great bulk of reportage and informed analysis of radical nationalism in Russia, and also of the primary source material constituted by the writings of the radical nationalists themselves, is available only in Russian. True, more or less competent secondary works in English and other Western languages do exist, but there are still not many of them, their coverage of the field is uneven, and they quickly grow out of date.[1] Any serious assessment still requires direct access to Russian-language sources. This means that only those with such access are in a position to make a *properly informed* contribution to discussion of the issues.

Given the political importance and sensitivity of the subject, this is—to say the least—not a very satisfactory situation. But a certain amount can be

---

1   This is certainly true of my own book, *Russian Fascism: Traditions, Tendencies, Movements* (New York: M.E. Sharpe 2001).

done to improve matters. Above all, it is essential to make the descriptive and analytical works of leading Russian[2] specialists on radical nationalism available in translation.

The book series *Soviet and Post-Soviet Politics and Society* is of significant value in this respect.[3] The study by Anastasia Mitrofanova of the Russian Orthodox wing of Russian nationalism[4] and the work of Vyacheslav Likhachev on political anti-Semitism[5] have already appeared, while Andrei Rogatchevski's book on the National-Bolshevik Party is forthcoming. The present volume makes available in English for the first time the systematic and detailed annual reports of current developments pertaining to radical nationalism in Russia prepared by specialists at the SOVA Center for Information and Analysis (Moscow).

The reports published here are those for 2004, 2005, and 2006, with some information relating to the first few months of 2007. As the corresponding reports for earlier years have not appeared in translation, the reader may feel the need for additional historical perspective. To what extent is the situation portrayed for the most recent period similar to the situation at earlier stages of Russia's post-Soviet development? What of significance, if anything, is really new? It may be helpful for me to offer an answer to these questions here. I am, I think, fairly well situated to do so, inasmuch as I was immersed in this subject matter while working on my book in the late 1990s and return to it now after a few years away, focusing on other issues.

It seems to me that very much remains basically the same as in past years. Thus, skinhead violence continues, and against the same set of victims—above all, racial and religious "aliens," but also leftists, homosexuals, members of rival youth subcultures, and the homeless.[6] Many of the changes that have occurred are of a kind that does not matter all that greatly. For ex-

---

2   I use the word "Russian" here, of course, in the civic (*rossiiskii*) and not the ethnic (*russkii*) sense.

3   http://www.ibidem-verlag.de/spps.html.

4   *The Politicization of Russian Orthodoxy: Actors and Ideas* (2005).

5   *Political Anti-Semitism in Post-Soviet Russia: Actors and Ideas in 1991-2003* (2006).

6   I leave aside the question of whether there is a clear upward trend in the scale of skinhead violence. The contention that radical nationalists are making increasing use of firearms and explosives also requires further verification.

ample, some ultra-nationalist organizations that played a prominent role in the 1990s—Russian National Unity is the obvious case—have fallen apart or declined in importance, while others have become more prominent (for instance, the National Imperial Party of Russia). The key point is that the radical nationalist scene is still fragmented, volatile, and divided along fault lines that also remain the same as before (ethnic versus imperial, Orthodox Christian versus neo-pagan, etc.). Nor do I see any fundamental change in the methods used by ultra-nationalists, ranging from electoral work and musical events to attract the young to the attempted usurpation of state functions and the skillful and rapid exploitation of local conflicts (as at Kondopoga) and other political opportunities that arise.

The main area in which recent years have seen striking change is that of the response to radical nationalism, both from civil society and from the state. That response has become much more vigorous. In addition, antifascist social forces have managed, to some degree at least, to overcome their internal divisions. On the whole, of course, these are hopeful developments, and all the more striking in the context of widespread political disorientation, disillusionment, and apathy. Yet here too there are grounds for concern, such as the rise of anti-fascist ("antifa") groups that use violent methods—and not only in self-defense.

The picture is especially mixed when we look at the response of the state. At long last, the police and procuracy, at least in some places, are taking strong action against hate crime and incitement to racial, ethnic, and religious hatred. More culprits are being prosecuted and jailed; more ultranationalist publications and websites are being closed down. It turns out, however, that these means are being applied selectively against opponents of the Putin regime. A case in point is the differential treatment meted out to the National-Bolshevik Party (NBP) and to the National-Bolshevik Front (NBF). The NBP has been treated much more harshly than the NBF, despite the fact that ideologically it is by far the more moderate of the two, because unlike the NBF it opposes Putin. An impression of determined official anti-fascism is thereby created to mislead the poorly informed observer, while in fact certain fascist elements are allowed to join the dominant coalition and influence state structures.

By making the excellent work of the team of specialists at SOVA available to a broader international readership, this book should help to raise the general level of debate about Russia and its future. The author, collaborators and translators are to be congratulated.

Stephen D. Shenfield
Providence RI, USA
October 2007

Preface

In 2007, *ibidem*-Verlag published the Russian version of a collection of quarterly reports[1] compiled by the SOVA Center.[2] This publication is *not* its English translation. The annual reports only partially overlap with the quarterly ones. Rather, the annual reports which are posted at the SOVA web site in the beginning of each year summarize the general situation assuming that the individual cases are already known to the reader from our daily *Xeno-News*, quarterly reports, or other sources, unrelated to SOVA, such as *The Russian Nationalism Bulletin* appearing biweekly since November 2007.[3]

Almost all individual facts that form the basis of the reports are also posted on the SOVA web site: http://sova-center.ru. Therefore, the web versions of our publications hardly have any references to sources. To simplify the reader's job, these references were added to the book version. All tables in the book were compiled by me on the basis of our monitoring efforts.

The texts of this book version and the web version are practically identical. However, the linguistic as well stylistic quality of the book version is higher, and some statistical data was updated according to what had became known by January 2008.

I am grateful to everyone who helped me to prepare this book. Alexander Verkhovsky edited all reports. Irina Savelyeva and David Szakonyi translated them into English. Maria Rozalskaya helped to edit the translation.

---

1   Galina Kozhevnikova, *Radikal'nyy natsionalizm v Rossii i protivodeystvie emu: Sbornik dokladov Tsentra "Sova" za 2004-2007 gg.* S predisloviem Aleksandra Verkhovskogo. Soviet and Post-Soviet Politics and Society 52 (Stuttgart: *ibidem*-Verlag 2007).
2   SOVA Center for Information and Analysis was founded in Moscow in 2002. It studies such topics as nationalism and xenophobia, hate crime and hate speech, relations between the churches and the secular society, political radicalism, and also the misuse of anti-extremism by government office holders. Findings of monitoring and research are published on the web-site http://sova-center (in Russian, but some publications are also in English). "Sova" literally means "owl".
3   http://groups.yahoo.com/group/russian_nationalism/.

Eugene Veklerov thoughtfully edited the English text for this publication once more.

I will be happy to receive comments or any other suggestions or ideas from the readers. Please, use for doing so SOVA's e-mail address: mail@sova-center.ru.

Galina Kozhevnikova
Moscow, Russia
January 2008

I. The 2004 Annual Report

1. Manifestations of Russian Nationalism

1.1. Organized Actions

In comparison with previous years, nationalist acts are becoming less and less isolated, but instead are acquiring a more systematic, organized, and public character.

Pickets organized by various activists of nationalist movements are becoming more regular, including those by the National Imperial (*derzhavnaya*) Party of Russia (NDPR), Party of Freedom, among others. In 2004, for the first time, these movements expanded their efforts to organize public meetings, a few of which were intended to be national in scale. Thus, on March 16, 2004 near the Gorky Park, a mass meeting was held by the Movement Against Illegal Immigration (DPNI), which was formed two years earlier after anti-Armenian pogroms in Krasnoarmeisk. Similar meetings by the same movement were held in St. Petersburg on March 16 and then again in Pskov on March 26.[1] However, law enforcement authorities dispersed a meeting organized by the Party of Freedom in Izhevsk.[2] Besides DPNI members, there were participants from NDPR, People's National Party (NNP of Ivanov-Sukharevsky) and others. These activists rallied under the slogans: "Terrorism Has an Ethnicity, and You Know It," "[Take Your] Suitcase – [Go to the] Train Station – [and Return to the] Caucasus," and "Moscow – A Russian City." Law enforcement authorities guarding the event, not only refrained from curbing the openly racist propaganda, but, on the contrary, arrested those ac-

---

1   "Dva desyatka tineydzherov protestovali v Pskove protiv nelegal'nykh immigrantov" (Twenty teenagers protested in Pskov against illegal immigrants). *Pskovskoe informatsionnoe agenstvo*, 6/3/04 (http://informpskov.ru/society/12712.html).

2   "Izhevskie natsionalisty pytalis' provesti nesanktsionirovannyy miting" (Izhevski nationalists tried to conduct an unsanctioned meeting). *IA REGNUM*, 17/3/04 (http://www.regnum.ru/news/233151.html?forprint).

17

tivists from leftist organizations, who had arrived, shouting slogans with the hope of disrupting the meeting.[3]

The March 16th event evoked widespread disgust in all of the major mass media outlets. Remarkably, these same news organizations failed to report an even more representative and well-attended right-wing action a month later on June 22. This latter June action claimed to protest against the spread of drugs in Russia. Organizers targeted migrants of non-Russian ethnicity as the primary cause of such criminal activities, even calling directly for pogroms to solve the perceived problem ("If you witness drug trafficking in your home, do not wait, while your children begin to start shooting up drugs - Take up sticks and fight!"). Under this pretext, State Duma Deputies from the fractions 'United Russia' (Evgeni Roizman) and 'Rodina' (Nikolai Pavlov) joined the activists in this meeting.[4]

Organizations under the name Russian National Unity Front (RNE) are gradually recovering after a long crisis (after a split in 2000, currently only two large-scale unions remained under such a name). For the first time in several years, there has been an explosion of RNE activities: in a number of cities in 2004 RNE leaflets were distributed calling for unity in armed self-defense.

The recent mobilization of nationalist groups has also displayed quite a new characteristic. These movements have begun to take public responsibility for all nationalist crimes and openly threaten antifascist activists. Although the majority of these declarations are only intended as PR moves, it is impossible to ignore the turning point in the behavior of Russian nationalists, who are now trying to break out of the narrow realm of marginal publications and websites.

In 2004, Alexei Kozlov, a member of the human rights movement of Voronezh, was beaten by nationalists, and violent threats were regularly directed at both activist Dmitry Krayukhin in Orel and the leader of the Youth

---

3   Sokolov-Mitrich, Dmitry. "Pervyy miting protiv terrora proshel pod natsionalisticheskimi lozungami" (The first meeting against terror used nationalist slogans). *Stolichnaya Vechernyaya Gazeta,* 17/03/04.

4   In the press release, it was reported that representatives of the Council of Federation, Moscow State Duma, and Moscow Government had also planned to participate in the meeting. However, reports from the meeting itself don't mention this issue. (pda.mednovosti.ru/corp/2004/06/22/miting/ and www.dpni.org/news.html# newsitem1087934890,73278).

human rights movement Andrei Yurov.[5] In December 2004, the National Socialist Group 88 claimed responsibility for the murder of the ethnic Georgian Dmitry Tarkeladze in Moscow.

As Russian nationalist groups openly declared a readiness for violent operations, two incidents in the Moscow region further displayed the increasingly radical nature of these movements. On May 25, 2004, in Dolgoprudny, the car of local judge Zhanna Radchenko was blown up, and a bit later on August 9th, another judge, Natalia Urlina, was murdered. In both cases the investigators link, as one of the possible versions, the crimes with the fact that both of the judges participated in a trial that had sparked the interest of local members of RNE.[6]

However, an even more alarming example is the murder of Nikolai Girenko, a scholar who participated as an expert in a series of trials against Russian nationalists. He was killed in St. Petersburg on June 19th, 2004, by a bullet shot through his apartment door. Literally a day after the killing, a certain dwarf organization named Russian Republic (headed by Vladimir Popov) came forward to claim responsibility, only to be followed by the co-chairman of NDPR Alexander Sevastyanov who publicly supported the act. Both of these proclamations, broadcast by Russian television channels, reached the homes of millions of Russians, giving that extra boost to the propagandizing efforts of the nationalists. At least, both statements were accompanied by commentaries by journalists.

Beginning in May 2004, the television channel TV-3 has aired the program "Our Strategy." This program has displayed a clearly nationalist character (mostly antisemitic), with Dmitry Rogozin, Andrei Savelyev, and Sergei Baburin, MPs from the 'Rodina' party, appearing as experts. It is indicative

---

5   "Natsisty ugrozhayut pravozashchtnikam" (Nazists threaten rights defenders). *Prava cheloveka v Rossii*, 23/8/04 (http://www.hro.org/actions/nazi/2004/08/23.php).

6   Activists of the RNE represent a "support group" of policemen who have been convicted of exceeding their authority in the arrest of Aliev. During one of the trial proceedings, they tried to organise a 'demarche,' and N. Urlina removed them from the courtroom. Radchenko blocked the action, contesting the judge's action to remove the members. Perekrest, Vladimir. "Sud'e, otklonivshey isk RNE, podlozhili bombu" (Judge who denied an RNE claim was bombed). *Izvestiya*, 28/5/2004 (http://main. izvestia.ru/print/?id=123325); Andryuhin, Alexander, Kirillov, Roman "Mafia ili

that "Our Strategy" attracted very little negative publicity, in contrast to the immediate public reaction to the very first episode of the program "Antideza" aired in 2002.[7]

Nationalist propaganda, albeit gradually, has openly penetrated into Russian public schools. As such, in May 2004, a scandal erupted surrounding the development of an all-Russian competition with the central theme of "What does it mean to be Russian?" The Russian Ministry of Education, although not having assisted the organizers of the contest, took no steps to prevent it from happening. Capitalizing on the popularity of rhetoric about the patriotic development of Russia's youth, the NDPR and Alexander Sevastyanov worked as organizers of the contest. At the same time, the State Duma Committee for Culture and Tourism was among the founders of the event. The final stage of the competition, which included around 600 entries from 60 regions of Russia, was held at the Moscow Humanitarian University (a former Komsomol school of higher education).[8]

1.2. Violence

The number of murders committed due to ethnic or religious hatred increased in comparison to the previous year. In 2004, we observed no less than 49 killings, as compared to approximately 20 in 2003. However, the figures we present here only reflect those crimes reported in the media, as well those where the motivation of the crime was unequivocally determined to be connected with hate. As a rule, these crimes have a variety of similar characteristics; for example, people of "non-Slavic" appearances are attacked on the street by a band of five or more youths. The victim is usually kicked and beaten with baseball bats, but, if less than five attackers are involved in the crime, knives are often used. Witnesses attest that the criminals also chant nationalist slogans throughout the attacks. At least ten additional murders had no such features (usually, as a result of the absence of any witnesses), but

---

natsisty" (Mafia or Nazis). *Izvestiya,* 11/08/04 (http://www.izvestia.ru/conflict/258379_print).
7   "Deza" is a slang term for disinformation.
8   "Chtoby spasti russkikh, nado sozdavat' partizanskie otryady" (In order to save Russians, we need to create partisan groups). *Izvestiya,* 19/05/04.

however, we believe with high probability that they may be classified as hate crimes. Among those killed by skinheads in 2004 were citizens from Afghanistan, Vietnam, Guinea-Bissau, Jordan, China, Korea, Lebanon and Syria. In particular, the murders of a citizen of Guinea-Bissau in Voronezh in February 2004 and of a Vietnamese citizen in October 2004 in Saint Petersburg caused large-scale protests by foreign students studying in Russia. The murder of Khursheda Sultonova, a girl from Tajikistan, similarly provoked a large public response in February 2004.

Furthermore, as a result of skinhead attacks, over 218 people were beaten or stabbed, resulting in varying degrees of injury to the attacked (not counting those involved in mass fights). Besides affecting Russians, these attacks targeted citizens from a minimum of 24 countries. We use the term "a minimum" because news about these incidents often describe the victims simply as foreign citizens. Moreover, these statistics are incomplete, since they fully rely on Russia media, which in no way covers all episodes of such violence. According to the 'Migration and Rights' Information Center supported by the 'Tajikistan' Foundation, taking into account only crimes which occurred in Moscow and Moscow region and affected only Tajiks, there are one to three attacks monthly which clearly display a hate motive and result in the death or serious wounding of the victim.

The main centers of violence were Moscow and the Moscow Region (17 murders, 62 beatings) and Saint Petersburg (9 murders, 32 beatings). However, the media coverage was much wider in both areas, partly lending to an explanation of why more were reported.

According to statistics collected by the Sova Center, following the two above-mentioned regions, Krasnodar region experienced the third highest number of attacks, where, not counting those involved in mass fights, two murders and 27 beatings were reported. In these cases, Cossacks, and not skinheads, appeared as the primary attackers with crimes against Meskhetian Turks. Many incidents of violence simply were not registered, not covered in the regional press, and consequently not investigated (as per information of the human rights organization Memorial, for the last 15 years not one crime against Turks has been brought to trial[9]). The clearest example of such lack of attention is the coverage by REN-TV, coinciding with the Day of Protection of Human Rights, whereby journalists reported on the cruel beating of 2 Turks by 5 unknown assailants (December 2). Law enforcement authorities began an investigation into the crime, but fingered one of the victims as the culprit of the assault.[10]

Apart from the two capitals and Kuban region, over 24 regions of Russia experienced some kind of nationalist violence, including Voronezh, Nizhniy Novgorod, Tyumen', Novosibirsk, Primor'e regions, and others.

Victims of a skinhead attack need not only be members of minority group such as black people and/or people from the Caucasus, customarily priority targets for attacks. Any non-Slavic appearance is enough to attract the attention of skinheads. For example, at the end of December 2003 in Saint Petersburg, an ethnically Nanai student was killed (according to different sources, this attack happened at the beginning of January 2004). In March in Orel, skinheads beat up members of the Buryatia and Chita region archery teams, who came to take part in a competition. One of the victims said afterwards, that even after they had been beaten by skinheads chanting, "Russia is for Russians," they were maliciously mocked for their non-Slavic appearance by both the doctors in the ambulance and in the hospital where they were taken.[11]

The wave of ethno-nationalist violence has again forced representatives of foreign countries to turn to the Russian government officials with public complaints. In January 2004, Henrik Sven Hirdman, the doyen of the diplomatic corpus, the Swedish ambassador to Moscow, expressed his discontent over the development of extremism in Russia.[12] In March, he announced his intentions to set up a meeting about rising xenophobia with the General

---

9   "V Krasnodarskom krae ubili dvukh turchanok" (In Krasnodar region, two Turks were killed). *Polit.ru*, 27/12/2004 (http://www.polit.ru/news/2004/12/27/mesh.html).
10 "24 chasa" (24 Hours) TV Program. *REN-TV*, 10/12/2004, 12:30 PM.
11 Getmanski, Konstantin, Mikeladze, Koba. "Zhertvoy skinhedov stali buryatskie strelki iz luka" (Buryatiski archers are victims of skinhead attack). *Izvestiya*, 1/4/2004.
12 "Duayen dipkorpusa v Moskve obespokoen proyavleniyami ekstremizma v Rossii" (Doyen of the diplomatic corps in Russia is troubled by manifestations of extremism in Russia). *Grani.ru*, 22/01/2004 (http://grani.ru/Events/Crime/m.57766.html).

Prosecutor of Russia Vladimir Ustinov, and also, if possible, with representative of the Ministry of Interior.[13] Also, on December 13, 2004, the Chinese embassy in Moscow warned its citizens in Moscow and in other cities about the need to take measures to safeguard personal safety in connections with recent attacks on Chinese citizens in Russia. At the same time, the foreign department of the Chinese government demanded that the Russian government take real and effective measures towards providing the personal security of Chinese citizens and their property.[14] It's not the first time when diplomats have come up with such statements. Two years ago a similar request was put forward to the Russian government and law enforcement authorities.[15]

We need to comment on a more characteristic trait of crimes by neo-Nazis. Their ideological position, which calls for a "struggle to purify the race," sanctions violence not only towards foreign nationals, but also towards 'anti-social' elements of society, in particular, homeless people.[16] Although attacks have also occurred in the past, it is significant that law enforcement authorities have stopped denying the neo-Nazi motivations behind the killings. In 2004, five such attacks, in which 13 people died, were reported in Moscow, Petrozavodsk, Krasnodar, and Khabarovsk.

As in previous years, in 2004, skinheads repeatedly organized large-scale destructive acts.[17] On January 26, the Orekhovsky Market was razed in Moscow. Fortunately, in notable contrast to the well known Tsaritsyno and

---

13 "Inostrannyy diplomaticheskiy korpus vstrevozhen rostom ksenofobii v Rossii" (Foreign diplomatic corps is alarmed by the growth of xenophobia in Russia). *Jewish.ru,* 04/03/2004.
14 (http://xeno.sova-center.ru/45A2A1E/4A69572).
15 Kozhevnikova, Galina. "Vozbuzhdenie rozni, prizyvy k diskriminatsii i nasiliyu na etnicheskoy i religioznoy pochve" (Fomenting hostilities, calling for discrimination, and violence towards ethnic and religious groups). *Prava cheloveka v regionakh Rossiyskoy Federatsii, 2002.* Moscow, 2003. pp. 235-236.
16 For example: Likhachev, Vyacheslav. *Natsizm v Rossii.* Moscow, 2002. pp.30-31.
17 We are not taking into consideration the pogrom in the Volgograd market in April 2004 and pogroms of Caucasian cafes in the fall of 2004 (as a result of which two people died). The police insist that both conflicts were just clashes of ethnic criminal groups. However, we would like to turn attention to the fact that during the trials in Volgograd, witnesses reported nationalist slogans by the gangs. In Ekaterinburg, the main suspects were teenagers who study at vocational schools (places where there are usually many skinheads).

Yasenevo pogroms in 2001, the Orekhovsky attack passed without victims; 20 young men armed with metal rods tore down several tents and fled when the police arrived. However, based on the fact that several skinhead groups denied any involvement in the assault and that witnesses failed to mention any nationalist slogans, investigators attributed the violence to "unmotivated aggression by intoxicated youths."[18] On the same day, skinheads organized a march through the streets of Vladivostok. In Izhevsk on the 23rd of February, supporters of the Party of Freedom beat up participants of an anti-war picket set up by left-wing youth. As a result of this attack, several people were injured.[19] At the beginning of March, skinheads participated in a mass fight at the People's Friendship University in Moscow. Injuries were reported, with there even being talk of murder.[20] On July 2, 2004, a crowd of up to 100 people, yelling nationalist slogans, ignited a pogrom against Caucasian cafés and stores in a village Tulun, Irkutsk region. One person was hospitalized as a result.[21] On the 22 of August, a group of skinheads charged an Armenian restaurant in Saratov, sending one person to the hospital as well.[22] Mass fights initiated by skinheads also erupted in Ekaterinburg, Arkhangelsk, Novosibirsk, and other regions.

The inaction of police has greatly contributed to the growth in racist violence, as exemplified by a pogrom against a Chinese dormitory in Vladivostok at the end of May 2004. As a result of the attack by skinheads, 10 people were injured, with one being sent to the hospital. Two security guards man-

---

18   "Nekontroliruemye. Na yuge Moskvy skinkhedy razgromili rynok" (Uncontrollable. In the south of Moscow, skinheads raid market). *Gazeta.ru,* 27/1/2004.

19   "Izhevskie neofashisty napali na anarkhistov, provodivshikh antiputinskiy miting" (Izhevsk neo-fascists attack anarchists who organized anti-Putin march). *IA REGNUM,* 23/02/2004 (http://regnum.ru/allnews/221574.html).

20   Zhimbueva, T. "Stolichnyy diplom i stolichnye shtuchki" (Diploma and things in the capital." *Molodyezh Byratii,* 17/03/2004. (Quoted from a report on the manifestations of xenophobia, racial discrimination, and anti-Semitism in the Republic of Buryatia – events from August 2003 to March 2004). (http://ngo.burnet.ru/hrcentr/rel2003-2004.html#_edn10).

21   "Irkutskaya oblast'. V Tulune uchinen pogrom, imeyushchiy, vozmozhno, natsional'nuyu podopleku" (Irkutsk region. In Tulun, a pogrom, having possibly a hidden nationalist motive, took place). *Regions.ru,* 06/06/2004.

22   Andreeva, Nadezhda. "Den' flaga otmechen pogromom v kavkazskom restorane" (Flag Day celebrated by pogrom in Caucasian restaurant). *Novaya Gazeta,* 26/08/2004 (http://2004.novayagazeta.ru/nomer/2004/62n/n62n-s10.shtml).

aged to prevent more serious injures to the residents, all the while as law enforcement authorities refused to break up the violence (the police called on
the perpetrators to cease the bloodshed themselves).[23]

Looking at the events of the last year, it has become more apparent
that "victims" are beginning to defend themselves from such assaults. As
such, in Novosibirsk, 13-year old Dzhanakhir Ramazakov was able to stand
up against 18-20-year old youths who attempted to beat him. At the end of
November, an Azerbaijani man stabbed two skinhead attackers in the Moscow metro. On December 18, a citizen from Tajikistan in self-defense stabbed
and severely wounded street muggers, as a result of which one died. It is also
highly likely that the arrest of a group of skinheads on November 17 occurred
as a consequence of strong resistance by Azerbaijanis to the assault by
these young men. This is a new development, as is the wider appearance of
protests by foreign students, which call for greater protection against racists.
In 2004, such public meetings were held in Voronezh, Saint Petersburg and
Moscow.

1.3. Spontaneous Conflicts

Besides the greater mobilization of nationalist organizations and skinheads, experts have also traced a growth of ethnic xenophobia among Russian citizens as a whole. Even the inaction by officials in such a complicated
situation is fraught with spontaneous interethnic clashes. The danger of pogroms against Chechens in Ingushetia after the raid of Basaev[24] and the real
threat of the resumption of Ossetian-Ingush conflict after the hostage situation
in Beslan[25] both appeared as direct consequences of the Chechen war. Only
efforts by local administrations, law enforcement officials, and civil society or-

---

23   Zhurman, Olga. "Okhranniki ostanovili krupnoe poboishche na rasovoy pochve"
      (Security guards stop large racial fight). *Nelegalov.net,* 28/03/2004.
24   "Respublika Ingushetiya. Mestnye zhiteli ugrozhayut pogromom lageryu chechen-
      skikh bezhentsev" (Republic of Ingushetia. Local residents threaten Chechen
      camp). *Regions.ru,* 24/06/2004.
25   For extra material, see Kolesnikov, Andrei. "Zhizn' posle smerti" (Life after death).
      Kommersant, 06/09/2004; the same author, "Kakaya doroga vedet k morgu" (What
      road leads to the morgue). Kommersant, 08/09/2004; and "Uydi, ty nas dostal" (Beat
      it, we've had enough). *Kommersant,* 09/09/2004.

ganizations prevented the outbreak of pogroms (in particular these organs were able to promptly evacuate all Chechen and Ingush students out of North Ossetia in the fall of 2004).[26] However, in 2004 a series of spontaneous inter-ethnic clashes was reported in regions far from the main war actions.

For example, in Chita region, the failure of a school administration to promptly resolve an ethnic conflict among school children led to a mass fight and a pogrom of the school by members of Dagestani community. Significantly, the majority of national journalists laid responsibility for the conflict only on the Dagestanis, even though the local press refuted this coverage.[27] In the Samara region, a longstanding 'frozen' conflict also came to surface between local residents and Azerbaijani community. The residents of the village Sukhie Avrali, complaining about the improper hygiene of the Azerbaijanis, led mass beatings against the Azerbaijanis, followed by arrests of the victims by the local police. As a result, by the beginning of spring 2004, the conflict was not solved, but the mutual resentment of the potential combatants continued to rise. To date, the local administration has not taken any steps to alleviate the underlying problems. A similar household conflict between residents of Malaya Purga in Udmurt Republic provoked pogroms against Azerbaijani restaurants and culminated in a mass fight that required the hospitalization of a number of people.[28] The Tajiki community in the village Shirokaja Rechka, Sverdlovsk region, did not wait for a pogrom. The Tajiks left the village on the eve of an "anti-narcotic" nationalist gathering of local residents, supported by sympathizers from Ekaterinburg.[29]

The overall impression from the situation is that officials (from school administrations to the governor's office), who are not able to fulfill their duty correctly and on time, find it more convenient to draw the people's discontent aside and to direct it to another channel. Absolutely ineffective and thought-

---

26   Petelin, German. "My ne mozhem garantirovat' im bezopasnost'" (We cannot guar-antee their safety). *Novye Izvestiya*, 18/11/2004.
27   Karpenko, Alexander. "Neizvestnyy istochnik soobshchaet" (Unknown source in-forms). *Zabaykal'skiy rabochiy*, 2004, No. 166.
28   "Zhizn' pereselentsev prevratilas' v ad" (Life of migrants is turning into hell). *Tele-company TVC*, 01/11/2004.
29   "Ekaterinburg. V poselke Shirokaya rechka ne ostalos' ni odnogo tadzhika" (Ekaterinburg. In village Wide River there is not a single Tajik left). *Regions.ru*, 07/05/2004.

less social reforms, the never-ending war in Chechnya, and the strengthening of terrorist activity in Russia have made it easy to target foreigners as "enemies".

1.4. Caucasophobia and Islamophobia

The war in Chechnya and the increased frequency of terrorist acts, particularly the Beslan siege, appear as two of the most important factors for the continuing growth of Caucasophobia and Islamophobia. This growth is reflected in poll data,[30] analyses of Russian mass media,[31] and our statistical research.

In particular, after the August terrorist acts on airplanes, a wave of people began to refuse to fly alongside other passengers of Caucasian or Muslim appearance. Representatives of airlines came to the side of the biased passengers and began illegally removing people from flights. At least four such cases were reported. The first occurred on September 1st on a flight from Sharm-al-Sheikh to Moscow, and the last on September 23rd on a flight from Moscow to Hurgada (Egypt). Not only Muslims and Caucasians were taken off the flights, but also people looking like such groups and people who stood up to oppose the practice. For example, in September on an Aeroflot flight to Canada, the crew removed a passenger who was actually an ethnic Ukrain-

---

30   For example, the Levada Center about nationalist sentiments of Russians. National-izm and Xenophobia - Sova Center. (http://xeno.sova-center.ru/45A2A39/47A071B).

31   For more information, Kozhevnikova G. "Yazyk vrazhdy v predvybornoy agitatsii i vne ee" (Language of Hostility within Election Campaigns and without them), 2004; "Yazyk vrazhdy v SMI posle Beslana: poiski vraga i otvetstvennost' zhurnalistov" (Hate speech in Mass Media after Beslan: Pursuit of the Enemy and the Responsibility of Journalists). *Natsionalizm i ksenofobiya*. Sova Center.

ian, because "he looked like a Chechen."[32] In St. Petersburg, it is also known that a hospital refused to treat of patient of "Caucasian" appearance.[33]

On September 18th, a mob of skinheads, chanting "This is for the Terrorist Acts!," beat up four passengers on the Moscow metro.[34] At the end of October, the corpse of a Tajiki construction worker was discovered with the words "Death to *Khach*[35] Death to Islam!" written across his body.

Many newspapers have covered the difficulties, experienced by women wearing a head-scarf (hijab) after the terrorist acts.[36] In Vladivostok in September, a group of skinheads attacked Muslim women, shouting "Shahidki (*female shahids*), get out from Primorie! We've had it with Beslan!"[37] In October 2004, Damir Mukhetdinov, the deputy chairman of the Muslim Religious Board for the Nizhniy Novgorod region even allowed local Islamic women not to wear headscarves "if it threatens their lives."[38]

In September of 2004 a group of radical Orthodox organizations sent a letter, full of grammatical mistakes, to President Putin and Moscow Mayor Luzhkov demanding "the introduction, in Russia and especially in Moscow, of

---

32   "Ne stoit slishkom sil'no zagorat' – vas mogut prinyat' za terrorista" (You should not get too much tan – you might be taken for a terrorist). *Vestnik Kipra*, 24/09/2004 (http://www.cyprusadvertiser.com/article.php?id=2467). About 'airo-Islamophobia": "Russkie turisty otkazyvayutsya sadit'sya v odin samolet s litsami, v kotorykh oni podozrevayut posobnikov 'islamskikh terroristov'" (Russian tourists refuse to sit on airplanes next to people who they suspect of being accomplices to 'Islamic terrorism'). *Religiya v svetskom obshchestve*. Sova Center.
33   "Meditsinskie uchrezhdeniya goroda ostayutsya pod usilennoy okhranoy" (Medical
34   Filatov, Konstantin "'Obychnye strizhennye molodye lyudi': skinkhedy izbili v metro priezzhikh s Kavkaza" ('Normal short-haired young people' – skinheads beat up Caucasian   immigrants).   *Vremya   Novostei,*   20/09/2004 (http://www.vremya.ru/2004/170/51/107922.html).
35   *Khach* is a derogatory term, usually meaning an ethnic Armenian, but sometimes it is applied to other non-Slavic ethnicities.
      More about this: "Moskovskie musul'manki opasayutsya poyavlyat'sya na ulitse v khidzhabe" (Moscow Muslims are scared to wear head-scarves in public). *Religiya v svetskom   obshchestve*.   Sova   Center,   28/09/2004   (http://religion.sova-center.ru/events/13B748E/43A77A5/441221B).
37   "Britogolovye napadayut na musul'man" (Skinheads attack Muslims). *Komsomol'skaya Pravda*, Vladivostok, 10/09/2004.
38   "Ya sovetuyu musul'mankam ne nadevat' khidzhab, esli eto ugrozhaet ikh zhizni" (I am advising Muslims not to wear headscarves if that threatens their lives). D. Mukhetdinov.   *Kreml*   (Nizhniy   Novgorod),   09/11/2004 (http://www.riakreml.ru/society/?17328).

strict visa regulations for individuals of Caucasian ethnicity, violating the laws of our Fatherland".

The actions of government representatives and law enforcement authorities have only encouraged further nationalist developments. Caucasian immigrants, as in the past, remain some of the main victims of police brutality. After practically every terrorist act, police resume general searches and random arrests of Chechens and Caucasians.[39] These activities are often accompanied by violence by the law enforcement authorities themselves. In September 2004, *Novaya Gazeta* reported that on August 31st, police officers beat up and killed Chechen Apti Ayubov, the son of a former officer of the KGB.[40] In September, police officers assaulted Magomed Tolboev, a cosmonaut awarded the Hero of Russia award, and later in October, a mechanic of Ingush ethnicity. In all of these cases the police officers were carrying out orders. An anti-Chechen hysteria began in Samara after an explosion in a market on June 4th, as a result of which 11 people died. General searches and arrests of Chechens and Ingushs incited mass protests against police brutality,[41] but just a month later, in July, official representatives of the Chechen-Ingush community were beaten by police.[42] In December representatives of the Chechen community of the Sverdlovsk region announced their intentions

39   Glazer, Susan. Za vzryvom v Moskve posledovali pritesneniya kavkaztsev (Oppression of Caucasians has Followed the Explosion in Moscow). *Inopressa.ru*, 24/06/2004.

40   Izmailov, Vyacheslav. "Kak sistema bor'by s terrorizmom porozhdaey ego" (How the fight with terrorism is spawning it). *Novaya Gazeta*, 09/09/2004. Yaroshevskiy Vitaliy "Vyyti na ploshchad'" (Exit onto the Square?), ibid. Yaroshevskiy Vitaliy "Nazhali na Vasil'evskiy spusk" (Pressed on the Vasili Slope), ibid.

41   "Uchastniki mitinga checheno-ingushskoy diaspory v Samare potrebovali soblyudeniya ikh konstitutsionnykh prav" (Participants of the meetings of the Chechen-Ingush Diaspora in Samara demand the protection of their constitutional rights). *Kavkazsky uzel*, 11/06/2004 (http://kavkaz.memo.ru/newstext/news/id/673 693.html).

42   Sergeev, Ivan. "'Eto zh ne militsiya, ne prosto tak sud zaderzhivaet'. Glava GUVD otritsaet izbienie chechentsev" ('This is not the police, not simply a judge arresting'. Head of the Ministry of Internal Affairs denies beating of Chechens). *Kommersant in Samara*, 17/06/2004.

to take law enforcement authorities to court for their unlawful searches and arrests.[43]

In February and March of 2004 in Moscow, parishioners were rounded up outside the Historical Mosque. [44] Anti-Muslim raids in Buguruslan were accompanied by direct threats by police ("The time will come when we will force you, "gololobye",[45] to kiss both crosses and icons").[46]

The rise in anti-Islamic sentiments also was exhibited in many acts of vandalism. In September 2004 hooligans broke a window in a mosque in Noyabrsk, and a mosque in Nizhniy Novgorod suffered several attacks as well in 2004. Muslim graves and cemeteries were repeatedly defiled in a range of regions in Russia, including Yoshkar-Ola, Kirov, and Obninsk (twice).[47]

1.5. Antisemitism

As in the past, attacks on Jewish cemeteries, cultural centers and synagogues emerged as one of the most widespread manifestations of antisemitism. The distribution of assaults on Jewish cemeteries spread across at least 6 regions. Arson attempts, pogroms, and other acts of vandalism against synagogues and Jewish cultural centers were noted in Chelyabinsk, Nizhniy Novgorod, Perm', Omsk, Ul'yanovsk, and other regions of Russia. On the night of June 30th in St. Petersburg, a plaster bomb was thrown at a

---

43   "Sverdlovskaya oblast'. Chechentsy podayut v sud na nachal'nikov rayonnykh UVD. (Sverdlovsk region. Chechens take regional police chiefs to court). *Regions.ru*, 10/12/2004 (http://www.regions.ru/sepnewsarticle/news/id/1703098.html).

44   "Musul'mane vozmushcheny proizvolom moskovskoy militsii" (Muslims upset over raids by Moscow police). *Religiya i obshchestvo*. Sova Center (http://religion.sova-center.ru/events/13B742E/150814B/32B17A1).

45   *Gololobye* (foreheaded) is a derogatory term for Muslims in Russia.

46   "Musul'mane obvinyayut rukovodstvo militsii g. Buguruslan i sotrudnikov RUBOP Orenburgskoy oblasti v tselenapravlennoy atake na priverzhentsev islama" (Muslims accuse Police Chiefs of Buguruslan and criminal police department [RUBOP] of Orenburg region of an intentional attack on followers of Islam). *Religion and Society*. Sova Center (http://religion.sova-center.ru/events/13B742E/150814B/49D7853).

47   We intentionally have not included in this list the pogrom on an Armenian cemetery on March 2nd, 2004, in the Krasnodar region, since we consider it not a manifestation of xenophobia, but the result of intentional political support of ethnic intolerance in the region, orchestrated by the regional administration.

synagogue. Moreover, in Balakovo (Saratov region), antisemitic posters were discovered twice, one of which was furnished with a plaster bomb. There were more serious incidents. On March 5th in Moscow, a building belonging to the study of Judaism in the CIS suffered an attack by an explosive device. Fortunately, no one was injured. After calls to punish the chairman of the Yoshkar-Olinsk Jewish community, on September 25th, someone made an attempt to kill his son. The youth was treated for knife wounds in a hospital.[48] On December 16th in Moscow, Israeli citizen Mikhail Yusupov was beaten by an unknown group of attackers, who shouted antisemitic slogans. A week later on December 23rd, Israeli Ephraim Malov suffered the same fate.

Moreover, one need not be Jewish to be a victim of an antisemitic hate crime. For example, on June 24th 2004 in Kostroma, an ethnic Russian was killed by unknown attackers shouting, "Get it, Jew!" In Tver, antisemitic slogans were written on the walls of an Orthodox chapel.

However as before, public pronouncements and publications remained the most widespread form of antisemitism.

Some of the more alarming examples of such activities include the mass distribution in Kaliningrad of an antisemitic "Bulletin of Russian Autonomy,"[49] the dismissal and introduction of charges according to Article 282 of the Vice-Governor of the Altai Republic Vladimir Torbokov for antisemitic speech addressed to Prime Minister Fradkov, and literally a month later, the appointment of Svatoslav Grigoriev, a well-known antisemite in the republic, to a similar post.

Even the recent legal situation surrounding the company Yukos was not free from an "antisemitic subtext": the dyad "Jewish – Oligarch" quickly strengthened in the minds in a part of Russian society as another element of social discontent. At the very beginning of the banking crisis (happening during the second half of May), meetings of "scammed investors" in Moscow

---

48 "V Mariy El soversheno pokushenie na syna predsedatelya Evreyskoy obshchiny" (In Mari El, an attempt occurs on the life on the son of the chairman of the Jewish community). *Antisemitismu.net,* 27/9/2004 (http://www.antisemitismu.net/site/site. aspx?SECTIONID=239038&IID=242701).

49 "Prokuratura Kaliningrada vozbudila delo protiv antisemitskoy gazety" (Kaliningrad Prosecutor files charges against antisemitic newspaper). *Antisemitismu.net,* 15/09/2004 (http://www.antisemitismu.net/site/site.aspx?SECTIONID=239038&IID=240805).

sometimes carried antisemitic slogans. Enraged people demanded authorities "restrain" and "kick out of Russia" "Abramovichs, Khodorkovskies, Vekselbergs and other Fridmans" who have gone too far.[50]

1.6. Other Religious Intolerance[51]

In 2004, almost every religious denomination suffered some kind of attack.

Orthodox churches, as a rule, were victims of robbery or non-ideologically motivated aggression of youth.[52] However, events were reported where self-professed Satanists went after such institutions. Such occurrences took place in Orel, Bryansk, Ulyanovsk, and other regions of Russia.

Attacks on Protestant churches showed unmistakable signs of religious intolerance and the open inclination to violence by those assaulters.

During 2004, prayer houses of Pentecostals were burned to the ground in the outer Moscow region of Podolsk in February and in the Yaroslavl region in December. In August, a Molotov cocktail was thrown through the window of an Evangelical Christian prayer house in Izhevsk. On November 23rd, in a Nizhniy Novgorod Adventist church, members of the local RNE created an uproar. The local community of Evangelical Christians in Tula sternly refuted the explanation of an explosion of a prayer house in 2004, which connected the events with typical criminal activities. This vandalism is very likely to have been incited by anti-Protestant informational policy, about which representatives of Protestant churches repeatedly expressed their indignation. Adventist believers in Nizhniy Novgorod are regularly subjected to defamation. Protes-

---

50   "Obmanutye vkladchiki vykhodyat na ulitsy Moskvy pod antisemitskimi lozungami" (Deceived investors take to the streets with antisemitic slogans). *Seventh Channel,* 25/05/2004 (http://www.7kanal.com/news.php3?id=62870).

51   For more about occurrences of religious intolerance and acts of vandalism related to religious or memorial sites, see the section "Extremizm" on the "Religiya v svetskom obshchestve" page at the Sova Center website " (http://religion.sova-center.ru/events/13B74CE/).

52   For example, commenting on the multitude of acts of vandalism by teenagers on Orthodox sites in the Orel region, a methodologist of a local educational institute of teachers, Anatoly Mishenko assumed that such behavior was caused by unnecessarily aggressive educational policy by the Russian Orthodox Church.

tant denominations are often depicted as "totalitarian sects" on national Russian television.

2.   Counteractions to Radical Nationalism

2.1. Activities of Civil Society Organizations

Nongovernmental organization in a wide range of regions in Russia led educational demonstrations, conferences, round tables, and seminars with representatives of the federal government and law enforcement authorities. The size of such activities varied – from regional events to national demonstrations. For example, a protest to celebrate the International Day of the Fight against Racism and Antisemitism, organized by the Youth Human Rights Movement together with the International Network against Racism (UNITED), quickly spread across more than 20 regions of Russia and spanned more than a week. Ten other regions were involved in the project "Counteractions to the Hate Speech," in which problems of overcoming negative ethnic stereotypes were discussed. Furthermore, gatherings of schoolchildren were held to clean Russian streets of fascist graffiti. The project "Campaign against Xenophobia and Antisemitism in multinational Russia" lasted more than a year and was led by the Moscow Bureau for Human Rights, the Moscow Helsinki Group, and UCSJ with support from the European Commission. For a year and a half, the "Civil Society" foundation also organized the national project "Overcoming Ethnic Discrimination, Racism, Xenophobia, Intolerance, and Extremism in Russia."[53]

Counteractions against extremism sometimes were quite spontaneous. Such events were rarely covered by the Russian mass media. Nonetheless, at least one extremist activity was broken up thanks to the strong resistance by ordinary citizens (at least according to the official version.) At the beginning of October, a festival of skinhead rock groups was canceled in the club

---

53   Results of the first year of the project presented on the site of the Foundation "Monitoring discriminatsii i natsional-extremizma v Russii" (http://www.fzgo.ru/i_malgrant.shtml).

"Estakada" on Ryazansky Prospect.[54] Two years earlier in March of 2002, skinheads held a demonstration on Ryazansky Prospect, even succeeding in blocking the street.[55] After a similar concert on September 18th, passengers on the Moscow metro were beaten.

However, the opportunities of civil society organizations to combat radical nationalism are limited, while the cooperation with government officials is difficult for various reasons.

2.2. Criminal Prosecution of Skinheads

As in previous years, the efforts of government at all levels to combat ethno-nationalist extremism were not really very logical.

On one hand, there are efforts to fight such nationalist manifestations. This can be seen from the number of trials of skinheads, which, in contrast to previous years, have now been considering racist and hate motives in the adjudication of suspects. The trial of the murderers of an African student in Voronezh most exemplified this new trend. However, in our opinion, the case demonstrates the lack of a concrete position by both the state and society towards this kind of crime. First, the impact of the trial was not caused by the murder itself, but instead by the large-scale protests by foreign students, thereby provoking an international scandal. Secondly, only this scandal forced society to turn its attention to the strained environment and the complete inaction by authorities to combat the problem in the region (in 2003 analyses indicated that in the Voronezh region xenophobic attitudes were steadily growing not only at the household level, but also were becoming an observed norm of regional politicians).[56] Thirdly, law enforcement authorities

---

54   Gusev, Anatoly. "Fashistov ne pustili na Ryazanskiy prospect" (Fascists were not allowed on Ryazansky Prospect). *Izvestiya*, 10/10/2004 (http://www.izvestia.ru/capital/506157_print).

55   Kozhevnikova, G. "Zapret na propagandu voyny, na podstrekatel'stvo k diskriminatsii i nasiliyu" (Ban on war propaganda, on instigation to discrimination and violence) in *Prava cheloveka v regionakh Rossiyskoy Federatsii 2002*. Moscow, 2003. P. 236. (http://www.mhg.ru/publications/1F38A05).

56   See in particular: Yagodkin, Alexander. "Novoe pokolenie vyderaet peysy? Iskali natsional'nuyu ideyu – nashli natsistskuyu" (New generation pulls out payot? They

up until the last moment insisted on the ordinary explanation for the crime; there was a fictitious story invented about a murder attempt on a girl committed by a dark-skinned man.[57] Fourthly, the changes in the position of the investigation and the court's decision show clear signs of shallow demonstrative campaigning, directed at the placation of public opinion and the resolution of other problems involving propaganda: the relatively quick proceedings (taking half a year) started with an attempt to minimize the racial underpinnings of the crime and finished with a sentence under Article 282 under a wave of official declarations calling for the preservation of interethnic peace in Russia, all under intense pressure after the tragic events in Beslan. To one degree or another, all of these features are relevant (no matter what the final sentence is) to all of the high profile cases connected with skinheads.

Nonetheless, it is impossible to deny the fact that the statistics about convictions are changing for the better. In 2004, the nationalist motive was cited in a minimum of nine sentences, but only meted out for *violent* crimes. Besides the case in Voronezh, there were four cases in Moscow, two more cases in St. Petersburg (one of which involved the murder of a Roma girl in the fall of 2003), a case of a threatened bombing of a synagogue in Novgorod in September 2003, and finally a case involving the beating of an Indian student in the Vladimir region. In 2003, only three such examples of sentences citing the hate motive were reported (there were only eight cases in total in 2003 which brought up the issue).[58] Prosecutions of racially motivated crimes are currently being processed in several regions, included the trial of a murdered nine-year old Khursheda Sultonova, the trial of the group "Schultz-88",

---

looked for a national idea and found a Nazi one). *Novaya Gazeta* 11-13/8/2003 (http://2003.novayagazeta.ru/nomer/2003/58n/n58n-s18.shtml).

57   For example, Alexander Tarasov affirms that the Voronezh region is a place where radical national groups are quite openly protected by the authorities. See Tarasov, A. "Porozhdenie reform: Britogolovye, oni zhe skinkhedy" (Creation of Reforms: Shaved heads a.k.a. skinheads). *Svobodnaya mysl-XXI* No. 5, 2000 (http://www.left.ru/2001/13/tarasov26.html).

58   We apologize for a regrettable mistake in the 2003 report. See Kozhevnikova, G "Zapret na propagandu voyny, na podstrekatel'stvo k diskriminatsii i nasiliyu" (Ban on war propaganda, on instigation to discrimination and violence) in *Prava cheloveka v regionakh Rossiyskoy Federatsii 2002*. Moscow, 2003. Pp. 81-96. The current report contains clarified data from the Institute of General Prosecutor office for 2003 about crimes in which the ethnic hatred motive was present.

and six more proceedings in Moscow, Primorie, Tymen, and other regions of Russia.

However, often the convictions of skinheads for violent crimes do not cite the hate motive. The Criminal Code contains a general penalty enhancement provision for the commission of crimes with such a motive. Several other articles of the code provide specific enhanced punishments for particular crimes, including murder and infliction of grievous and moderate bodily harm, committed with these motivations. For example, in 2003, a group of teenagers disrupted the peace in the Moscow metro station Fili, as a result of which one policeman was murdered. On August 3, 2004, the Moscow Criminal Court sentenced the eight accused to terms of 4.5 to 18 years in prison with no hate motive cited in the verdict.[59] Happening two years after the crime itself, the sentencing of suspects for a pogrom in Yasenevo bewilders any observer. Of the five suspects, three were sentenced, all for hooliganism. Jurors recognized their leniency, in spite of the fact that one of the accused had been already convicted for a pogrom at a market in Tsaritsyno. As a result, the Moscow Criminal Court sentenced Andrei Pochukaev and Evgeni Serzhantov to two and a half years of probation, and Valeri Rysakov to six months of prison.[60] In 2004, similar sentences were handed out also in Tula, Lipetsk, Kursk, and no less than six other regions in Russia. However, we must admit that such a judicial practice already doesn't dominate sentences with "nationalist" motivation, as it was in previous years.

The relatively soft and rare convictions of skinheads, who systematically use violence to perpetuate racial hatred, stand in a remarkable contrast with the tough convictions handed out to members of the National Bolshevist Party (NBP). Not in any way denying the societal danger of the NBP's ideology, we cannot justify the extremely repressive measures taken against political hooliganism of NBP. For example, on December 20, seven NBP activists were

---

59 "Osuzhdeny uchastniki pogroma na stantsii 'Fili'" (Participants of the pogrom at metro station 'Fili' convicted). *Novye Izvestiya.* 4/8/2004 (http://www.newizv.ru/news/?id_news=8909&date=2004-08-04).

60 Fedocenko, Vladimir. "Sud prisyazhnykh: troe vinovnykh: Vchera vynesen prigovor po delu o pogrome na stolichnom rynke" (Jury: Three are guilty. Yesterday, a sentence was handed down in the case of a pogrom at a market in the capital). *Rossiyskaya Gazeta*, 28/02/2004 (http://www.rg.ru/2004/02/28/prigovor.html).

sentenced to five years in prison, only for taking over the office of the Minister of Health and messing up a few things. Two days later, 40 participants in a similar seizure of the reception of the Administration of the President were charged with an attempt to overthrow the government (?!) which can lead even to longer terms. Moreover, it is impossible to justify the rough treatment of NBP activists during and after arrest. Many observers have commented that the repression against the NBP has replaced actions to combat the more dangerous ethno-nationalist groups. Besides, a similar situation is happening with regards to a mass of investigations of real and presumed members of the Islamist organization "Hizb ut-Tahrir." This organization runs dangerous anti-democratic, fundamentalist activities, which is in no way connected to terrorism that is incriminated to its members.[61]

2.3. Counteractions to Organized Ideological Groups and the Propaganda of Radical Nationalism

If nationalist violence meets the resistance of the law enforcement authorities, even without proper qualifications of crimes, then the situation surrounding counteractions to ideologically consolidated groups and nationalist propaganda is quite different. In this respect, the state has done practically nothing to combat nationalists.

Similarly, concerns are completely justified about the danger of "inertia" of the law "Counteractions to Extremist Activities, especially regarding the part affecting nationalist, extremist alliances. Just as in 2002 and 2003, only one organization of this sort was disbanded under this law in 2004. Carried out under a court order in Omsk, the organization "Slavic Community Vedy Kapische of Perun" was dissolved for disseminating racist propaganda and using swastikas as symbols.[62] NDPR faced a similar situation when it tried

---

61   Ponomarev, Vitaly. "Bor'ba s radikal'nym islamom v Rossii: sila ili pravo" (Fight with Radical Islam in Russia: Strength or Right?) in *Predely svetskosti.* Moscow, Sova Center (will be printed in February). See also the selection of news on the site "Religiya v obshchestve" (http://religion.sova-center.ru/search?words=%D2%E0%F5 %F0%E8%F0).

62   Three legal entities representing one organization were invalidated. See: "Uchenye takoy religii ne znayut: Omskiy oblastnoy sud prinyal reshenie o likvidatsii ob'edineniya staroverov" (Scholars don't know that kind of religion: Omsk regional

unsuccessfully to appeal the decision of the Ministry of Justice about the abo-
lition of its registration (for formal reasons). The ministry's decision was upheld, and in October 2004 an arrest warrant was put out for one of the leaders of the party Boris Mironov, accused of incitement to nationalist hatred.

In the remaining cases, other formalities were used to justify the liquidation of organizations. In May 2004, under the initiative of the Justice Ministry
in the Vladimir region, the local departments of organizations 'Russian National Union' (RONS), 'Russian National Movement' (RND), and the 'Russian
National Unity' (RNE) were closed for incorrect tax declarations and reports
about activities. In August, the Naberezhnye Chelny city office of the Tatar
Social Center (TOTs) was also dissolved for similar reasons, as well as the
office of the 'Eurasia' party in October in Novgorod region and the Pskov office of the Party of Freedom in December.

Only the case of the TOTs actually can be interpreted as an action
against radical nationalism. This liquidation only occurred after a failed attempt in April 2004 of a prosecutor trying to convict the director of TOTs, Ra-
fis Kashapov of incitement to hatred by trying to destroy an Orthodox chapel
in 2003.

In Novgorod, besides the disbanding of the 'Eurasia' department, at
least six other regional departments of organizations were dissolved, following a large-scale inquiry by the Ministry of Justice (including offices of the
Council of Federation Speaker Sergei Mironov's 'Party of Life,' Gennady Se-
leznyov's 'Party of the Renaissance of Russia,' the Russian Communist
Worker's Party (RKRP), and others).[63]

In Vladimir, the liquidation of three active nationalist organizations was
accompanied by information that the regional Ministry of Justice had paid
close attention to other party organizations (in particular 'Party of Life'), which
was connected with the unofficial beginning of campaigning for the election

---

court decides to liquidate union of 'Old Believers'). *Otkrytyy Omsk,* 29/7/2004 (http://
www.regions.ru/article/any/id/1587892.html).

63   In total, 33 cases were filed. In the Novgorod region, a regional branch of the Eura-
      sia Party was liquidated. *Novgorodinform.ru,* 22/10/2004 (http://www.novgorod
      inform.ru/power/3408.html).

(the elections for Governor of the Vladimir region should have been held in March of 2005).[64] Representatives of the Ministry of Justice have claimed that the Pskov office of the Party of Freedom was also dissolved as a result of a large inspection of social organizations in the region.[65] However, the case draws more attention to itself, due to the fact that the court's decision was handed down amidst a scandal involving nationalist threats from this party, according to the version of the investigation, directed at Valentina Matvienko.

Counteractions against nationalist propaganda in the mass media haven't fared much better. Up until spring 2004, control over such publications lied not only in the hands of the prosecutor's office, but also in the Ministry of Printing. However, following the so-called 'administrative reform' passed during the fall of 2004, this work was practically paralyzed. If in 2003, the Ministry for Printing issued at least 35 warnings to mass media outlets for inflaming nationalist sentiments, then in 2004, we only know of one case of a similar warning by the Federal Agency for the Legal Supervision in the Sphere of Mass Communication and the Protection of Cultural Legacy.[66] At the end of December 2004, the newspaper 'North Ossetia' was warned for publication of an article entitled "The Beslan Tragedy Opened the World's Eyes to Ossetia."

On May 5, 2004, the head prosecutor of the Republic of Altai issued a warning against the unacceptable violation of the Federal Law "On Counteraction to Extremist Activities" by the newspaper 'Postscriptum' for the publication of an antisemitic article by the vice-governor of the republic Yu. Posdeev.

---

64   Novozhilova, Nataliya. "Na karte Vladimirskoy oblasti stalo men'she korichnevykh pyaten" (There are fewer brown spots on the Vladimir Region map). Internet Newspaper *"Tomix"* (Vladimir), 24/05/2004 (http://www.tomiks.vtsnet.ru/tomiks/scripts/ secondpg.cgi?0+0+0+0+0+detail-9547).

65   In Pskov region, a judge liquidated Party of Freedom. *Pskov Information Agency*, 21/12/2004 (http://informpskov.ru/print/17671.html).

66   The situation is not completely clear with regards to the Voronezh municipal newspaper "Bereg", in which a local branch of the ministry detected signs of national discord. However, no warnings were reported. "The Tsentral'no-Chernozemnoe Territorial Ministerial Government for Printing, Television, and Mass Media detects signs of incitement to national hatred in the publications of the Voronezh daily *Bereg*". *Religiya v svetskom obshchestve*. Sova Center (http://religion.sova-center.ru/events/ 13B748E/14DEEB8/3F5F391).

In 2004, a number of verdicts were passed down against nationalist mass media and their publishers.

Of the four convictions, only one banned the further publication of the accused media outlet (*Russian Veche* in Novgorod), and only after the first sentence was thrown out by a higher court. In the remaining three cases – *Izhevsk Division* of Mikhail Trapeznikov, *Russian Siberia* of Igor Kolodezenko and *Rusich* of Viktor Korchagin – the nationalist publishers were given probationary sentences, in spite of the fact that Kolodezenko and Korchagin had already been convicted earlier for similar offenses. Korchagin's case was later reversed by a higher court and will be retried. Not one of the convicted was banned from continuing their publishing activities, however illegal the publications were.

Furthermore, in May 2004, the case concerning nationalist publications against Yuri Belyaev, the leader of the Party of Freedom, was thrown out "due to the expiration of the statute of limitations."[67]

In January 2004, the leader of Khabarovsk office of the National-Sovereign Party of Russia (NDPR) was taken to court under article 282 for the publication of the second issue of the newspaper *Nation*. In 2003 he was given a two year suspended sentence for the publication of the first issue of the paper. Nothing more has come out as of yet about the judicial process.

In November 2004, legal proceedings were initiated against the radical nationalist newspaper *Our Fatherland*. It is worth noting that this occurred only against the backdrop of the campaign "for the protection of foreign students" in St. Petersburg. In August of 2004, rights defenders Ruslan Linkov and Yuri Vdovin had tried to initiate the same case and send it to court, but their efforts were denied.

---

67   Warning about the unacceptability of breaking the Federal Law 'On counteractions to extremist activities'" Prosecutor of the Altay Republic Official Site. (http://www.prokuratura.gorny.ru/News/vitovcev.htm).

2.4. Other Actions by the Government

We have seen efforts by the government to counteract open violence (particularly by skinheads) and increased support for declarations about the unacceptability of xenophobia at the highest levels of the state. Repeated statements by President Putin affirm this notion. In 2004, for the first time, the MVD publicly and officially recognized the presence of skinheads in Russia.[68]

However, in light of this, there has lacked a consensus at the state level about how to stabilize ethnic conflicts in Russia. Moreover, in 2004 the only federal program completed ahead of time was the Federal Program "Formulation of an Environment of Tolerance and the Prevention of Extremism in Russian Society." Sociologists further note, that at the local levels of government in many regions of Russia, government officials have acquired expertise and experience over many years in overcoming ethnic conflicts (see Perm' region).[69]

Unfortunately, the tendency to deny problems of radical extremism has not disappeared in Russia. For example, Valentina Matvienko stated that attacks on foreign students were not attacks by skinheads, but *"banditry and hooliganism."*[70] In 2003, in a conversation with American diplomats she also equated skinheads with pickpockets.[71] The deputy Minister of Culture for the Interethnic Relations Leonid Nadirov also holds similar opinions about such manifestations. He, in particular, has claimed that in the last few years in St. Petersburg, there has been only one crime motivated by nationalism – the

---

68   Fedosenko, Vladimir. "Skinkhedov pereschitali" (Skinheads recounted). *Rossiyskaya Gazeta*, 03/03/2004.

69   Mukomel, Vladimir. "Ksenofobiya ne tol'ko pryamoe fizicheskoe nasilie" (Xenophobia is not only physical violence). *Nationalism and Xenophobia*. Sova Center, 03/12/2005. (http://xeno.sova-center.ru/45A2A39/470A66B); Neganov, S.V. "Novoe v programmnom podkhode k razvitiyu natsional'nykh i mezhnatsional'nykh otnosheniy na regional'nom urovne" (New things in the approach to the development of national and international relations at the regional level). Center of International Cooperation (http://www.interethnic.org/News/291104_5.html).

70   "V. Matvienko denies the connection of extremist groups to the murders of foreigners in Saint Peterburg." *Natsionalizm i ksenofobiya*. Sova Center, 29/10/2004 (http://www.xeno.sova-center.ru/45A2A1E/46A2D3D).

71   Kozhevnikova, G. Zapret na propagandu voyny, na podstrekatel'stvo k diskriminatsii i nasiliyu." (Ban on war propaganda, on instigation to discrimination and violence). *Prava cheloveka v regionakh Rossiyskoy Federatsii, 2002*. Moscow, 2003. P. 91.

murder of an Azerbaijani watermelon trader in 2003. All of the rest – *"these are not our prerogative, these concern the MVD more, because all of them fall under hooliganism. You can call them skinheads, you can call them Chechens, you can call them individuals of Caucasian ethnicity, but they are all united until the criminal codex under which they operate."*[72]

Sometimes the refutation of nationalist crimes by officials comes across as direct provocations towards the further growth of xenophobia. Commenting on the wave of attacks against foreign students in the fall of 2004, the head of St. Petersburg police (GUVD) announced, that foreigners themselves were guilty for the cruelty of the assaults, since they had tried to resist the attacks (while in the notorious brochure "How Not to Become a Victim of Crime," written for foreign students studying in St. Petersburg in November 2004, the *police themselves recommended* that one offer resistance during encounters with skinheads). In addition, the boss of the GUVD claimed that *"the activities of extremist groups in the city are few,"* and foreign students living in St. Petersburg, *"themselves exaggerate the existence of extremism, demanding special protection"* and *"at times committing illegal acts"*[73] (few consider the first remark an appropriate estimation, the second doesn't deserve any commentary, and the last is in no way connected to the conversation).

Legislative initiatives in 2004 directed at overcoming nationalist manifestations elicit nothing but bewilderment. As an example, St. Petersburg demonstrated a full cycle of "organized campaigns" to fight xenophobia. The cycle began in the beginning of September after the tragic events in Beslan and following the announcement by Putin, which mentioned the unacceptability of fomenting national hatred.[74] At the time, the clearly declarative city law

---

72   "Zamestitel' ministra Leonid Nadirov predpochitaet ne zamechat' natsionalis-ticheskikh proyavleniy" (Deputy Minister Leonid Nadirov prefers not to notice nationalist manifestations). *Natsionalizm i ksenofobiya.* Sova-Center, 12/4/2004 (http://xeno.sova-center.ru/213716E/213988B/3627A95).

73   "'Inostrantsy sami vinovaty', - tak schitaet militseyskoe nachal'stvo Piterburga" (Foreigners are themselves guilty" – considers the police headquarters of Saint Petersburg). *Natsionalizm i ksenofobiya.* Sova Center (http://www.xeno.sova-center.ru/45A29F2/4A15D52).

74   Putin, V. "Zayavlenie na soveshchanii v operativnom shtabe po osvobozhdeniyu zalozhnikov" (Statement at the operational meeting about the liberation of hostages). *Official site of the President of the RF* (http://president.kremlin.ru/appears/2004/09/04/0645_type63374type63378type63381_76262.shtml).

"About International Relations in St. Petersburg" was passed. A little while later, after the murder of a Vietnamese student and spontaneous student demonstrations, Governor V. Matvienko claimed that there were no national-ist crimes in St. Petersburg. Instructions were then given to develop a city-wide program to increase tolerance and a special consultative committee was created. Extraordinary, almost comical publications were distributed to foreign students about "interactions with skinheads" and no less surprisingly (al-though henceforth not humorous), a special police department was created to provide the safety of foreign students...and exposure of illegal immigrants.

In November 2004, it was announced that from January 1st, 2005, a new city program developed by the Moscow city government would begin, entitled " Multinational Moscow: The creation of an atmosphere of interethnic solidarity, world culture, and nonviolence in the capital from 2005-2007." In spite of the fact that the main decision of the development of such a program was made back in 2001, this project would not be put into effect until March 2005.[75]

In September, deputies of the State Duma discussed the idea of changes to the Codex of Administrative Legal Offenses (KoAP). These changes would affect articles about culpability for "for the public harassment of any ethnicity or religion."[76] In essence, such an article in the KoAP might have been a realization of the last and the most indistinct paragraphs of the definition of extremist activities under the 2002 anti-extremism law. No further movement of this idea has happened, but it is easy to predict that such an article would be absolutely useless from the enforcement point of view.

---

75   "Rasporyazhenie pravitel'stva Moskvy ot 15 noyabrya 2004 g." (Directives of the Moscow Government from 15 November 2004). *Official Site of the Moscow City Government*   (http://www.mos.ru/cgi-bin/pbl_web?vid=2&osn_id=0&id_rub=2044& news_unom=35728).

76   Vinogradov, Mikhail. "My utratili kontrol' za dvizheniem naseleniya" (We lost control over the movement of population). *Izvestiya*, 15/09/2004.

3. The "Nationalist Resource" in Politics

3.1. Nationalist Actions by Representatives of Government

A whole row of officials have demonstrated their willingness to support nationalist initiatives or even come up with their own ones. We have already mentioned the participation of deputies from "United Russia" and "Rodina" in the nationalist meeting on June 22nd. In addition, twice in 2004, an attempt was made to revive an old bill by the Deputy of the Moscow City Duma Yuri Popov. In the press, this law was presented as having local jurisdiction, limiting migration into Moscow. Moreover, the deputy himself introduced the bill as a city initiative. In reality, there were two federal bills, intended to change the Russian laws "On the right of citizens of the Russian Federation to free movement and choice of residence within the boundaries of the Russian Federation" and "On the legal position of foreign citizens in the Russian Federation."

Both bills, in particular, foresaw new limits on citizens moving into territories, *"where as a result of the relocation of citizens arriving from other regions, a threat has emerged to the ethnic demographic balance in connection with the changes of the national makeup of the population, that has appeared in a significant, more than 10%* [for foreigners 5% - G.K.], *decrease of the share of size of the population representing one of these nations, whose size comprises no less that one third of the total population,"* and *"where as a result of arrival of citizens from other regions, a threat has emerged concerning the general deterioration of the* sense of ethnic well-being [emphasis mine, G.K.], *the weakening or loss of the ethnic spiritual, cultural, religious, and traditional national values representatives of one of those ethnicities, whose numbers comprise more than one third of the total population.*[77]*"* More than a third of the substantial part of both bills openly defines ethnicity as a deciding factor at the limiting of the freedom of movement.

Moreover, if in the spring this legislative attempt amounted to nothing but puzzlement, after Beslan in the fall of 2004, the renunciation of this bill

---

77   Texts taken from the official site of Deputy Popov [http://www.duma.mos.ru/cgi-bin/pbl_web?vid=2&osn_id=0&id_rub=781&news_unom=12201%20LINK=].

was in no way clear. Thus, the chief of the Moscow City Duma Committee for Economic Politics Irina Rukina came out in support of the bill, putting forth her argument that "*diasporas are robbing Moscow,*" and foreign migrants are provoking xenophobia themselves, since "*Muscovites every day envy the growing wealth of guest workers.*"

After the events in Beslan, the governor of the Moscow region expressed his support for the necessity of a complete inspection of citizens arriving in the region, especially from the Caucasus, though emphasizing that he was not speaking about ethnicity, but rather about the region of origin.[78]

In a few other regions, officials have either openly announced their preparedness for violent ethnic-nationalist actions, or put this intention into practice.

The front-runner of such official ethno-nationalist initiatives certainly remains the Krasnodar region. The main target, as in the past, is the Meskhetian Turks, in spite of the fact that the actions of the region's administration to put pressure on the Turkish population have been effective. A program shameful for Russia to relocate Meskhetian Turks to the USA began in 2004. However, this did not protect the targeted community from violence. The year began with the beating of three resident of Abinsk city, and ended with a mass fight on December 18th, as a result of which around 35 people were wounded. In addition, two Turkish women were cruelly murdered on December 26th.

The Meskhetian Turks are the main, but not the only target of the local government. The region's administration is purposefully fighting with all migrants of non-Russian ethnicity, regardless of Russian law. For example, in summer of 2004, the scandalous law "On arrival and residency in the territory of the Krasnodar region"[79] was finally abolished (two years after it had been passed). However, almost immediately, a new law was passed on July 2nd,

---

78   "V Podmoskov'e nachinaetsya total'naya proverka kavkaztsev i formirovanie narod-nykh druzhin" (In the Moscow region, a complete check has begun of Caucasians as well as the creation of national brigades). *Polit.ru,* 20/09/2004 (http://www.polit.ru/news/2004/09/10/gromov.html).

79   Legal analysis of this law, done by the Independent Expert Legal Council, can be found on the site "Human Rights in Russia": (http://www.hro.org/docs/expert/krasnod.htm).

titled "On measures about the prevention of illegal migration to Krasnodar region," and on July 20th the governor issued a decree with the same title. Both documents (in which not only foreigners, but also Russian citizens without registration, are considered illegal immigrants) have the same overly discriminatory character as the previous law and they contradict the Russian Constitution.[80] The regional prosecutor has contested both.[81] Meanwhile, as before, the federal government has not bothered to condemn the politics of the regional government.

At the end of 2004 in Kuban, filtration camps for "illegal" immigrants began to operate with the approval of the governor. These camps fall somewhere in between ethnic ghettos and concentration camps. At the beginning, it was planned that the camps would be located on the territories of former army bases, and migrants would live in the repaired barracks. However, only 5 million of the planned 24 million rubles actually found its way to the construction of the camps. As a result, the first such camp, opening in December 2004, came about as a tent city with a dining room and a lavatory (the tents were equipped with village flooring and small stoves). Surrounded by a barbed wire fence, the camp is 100 meters long and 150 wide. The distribution of the migrants was to be determined by ethnicity. How this was to be done was unclear. Statements of the regional officials let us assume that illegal immigrants will be put into these camps without any court decisions, which is a direct violation of the Federal Law (paragraph 9 article 30 Federal Law "On the rights of the foreign citizens in the Russian Federation"). We should add that the construction of these camps is made possible by the labor of illegal immigrants, which is also illegal.[82]

80   Legal analysis of this acts, done by the Independent Expert Legal Council, can be found on the site "Migration and Right" (Section "Publications, speeches, opinions") (http://refugees.memo.ru/For_All/rupor.nsf/ff1553f7545beb8ec3256a4c0038aceb/b8 5c325196b3cf4ac3256f710062b718!OpenDocument).

81   Fore more on discrimination in the Krasnodar region, see the report draft "Sistematicheskoe narushenie prav cheloveka v Krasnodarskom krae podryvaet mezhdunarodnyy avtoritet Rossii" (Systematic violations of human rights in the Krasnodar region undermine the international authority of Russia). *IA REGNUM*, 01/12/2004 (http://www.regnum.ru/news/369368.html).

82   "V Krasodare otkryli lager' dlya Gastarbayterov" (A camp for guest workers is opened in Krasnodar). *TV-Tsentr*, 23/12/2004; "Vremennye palatochnye lagerya dlya migrantov na Kubani mogut stat' postoyannymi" (Temporary tent camps for mi-

The idea of ethnic ghettos for migrants unexpectedly reverberated across Russia in the fall of 2004. Beside the Krasnodar governor, business-men from St. Petersburg (albeit anonymously) supported the concept during a round table discussing "Problems and Mechanisms of the naturalization and social adaptation of Migrants," organized by the regional fund "Gold Ten" in October 2004.

In other regions, similar activities have been organized to "push out" people of non-Russian ethnicity. For example, this happened in the city Revda, in Sverdlovsk region. In September of 2004, the head of the Sverd-lovsk organization 'Azerbaijan' Asad Kuloev announced that under joint ac-tions of the local government and police, all Azerbaijanis had been forced out of the region: "*Only three Azerbaijani men who have Russian wives remain there. But it is not safe there for them. Some officials call on the wives to di-vorce their husbands in order to expel the Azerbaijanis completely. When the women refused, they planted a rifle on one of my compatriots, and now he sits in SIZO (pre-trial detention facility).*"[83] The organization "Roma-Ural" ac-cused policemen of an anti-Roma pogrom, organized in Revda on the night of the 26th of August. Under the premise of a search for a murderer, the police and OMON (Special Police Unit) members (assumed to be intoxicated) wrenched open doors, burst into Roma houses in the city, and arrested and beat many people (including women and children). As a result of the raid, one person was hospitalized; local medical centers refused to treat the rest of the wounded.[84]

---

grants in Kuban may become permanent). *IA REGNUM* 27/12/2004 (http://www.regnum.ru/news/382336.html); "A. Tkachev posetil pervyy v krae depor-tatsionnyy lager'" (A Tkachev visited the first deportational camp in the region). *Yuga.ru*, 29/12/2004 (http://www.yuga.ru/news/45006/index.html).

83   "Ekaterinburgskaya militsiya ne usmotrela v pogromakh priznakov natsional'noy vrazhdy" (Arsons are clear criminal acts. Ekaterinburg police have not detected signs of national hatred in regions). *Samara Segodnya*, 11/09/2004 (http://news. samaratoday.ru/showNews.php?id=32911).

84   "Proishestviya v Revde" (Occurrences in Revd). *Roma-Ural*, 01/09/2004 (http://www.romaur.ru/news/news.html).

3.2. The "Nationalist Resource" in Elections

The use of xenophobic sentiments as an electoral strategy is becoming clearer. This has affected elections at all levels – from municipal to the State Duma and the President.

For now, with rare exceptions (it may as well be that we know little about the situation), the use of this resource has been only limited to aggressive ethno-nationalist rhetoric. At any rate, we know of only one case when someone claimed his willingness to use skinhead groups ("reoriented towards other aims") in the campaign events. At the time of the mayoral elections in Vladivostok in May of 2004, one of the candidates, former policeman Dmitry Dmitriev, publicly announced this intention.[85]

Moreover, deputy of the Yaroslavl region Duma Sergei Krivnyuk volunteered to head anti-Roma pogroms under the premise that Roma people were responsible for drug trafficking in the region. As soon as this statement was covered in the press, regional offices of the State Drug Control Agency and the Ministry of Interior publicly came forward with a statement that the involvement of Roma people in drug trafficking in the region was insignificant.[86]

In the Sverdlovsk region, the activities of the fund "City without Drugs" are not slowing down. This organization is headed by State Duma Deputy Evgeni Roizman from "United Russia", which is known for its violent methods of combating drug dependence. In 2004, members of the fund concentrated their efforts on the eviction of Tajiks from Yekaterinburg and the surrounding region, accusing them of drug trafficking (incidentally, even the newspaper *Rossia*, known for its publication of ethnically inflammatory articles, commented on "the nationalist tinge" of the fund's activities). The situation could not go down without a scandal: the fund expressed its intentions directly to the Tajikistani Ambassador to Russia Safar Safarov. As an answer, the director of the Tajik cultural center "Somon" in the Sverdlovsk region Farukh Mirzoev turned to the prosecutor's office with a demand to initiate legal proceed-

---

85   Usova, Margarita "Schitayte menya sumaschedshim" (Consider me crazy). *Zolotoy Rog* (Vladivostok), 11/05/2004, No. 35 (http://www.zrpress.ru/2004/035/g011.htm).

ings against the leadership of the fund for incitement to national hatred.[87] As of now, we don't know if the process has been undertaken.

Anti-Caucasian propaganda was actively used during electoral campaigns for governor in the Pskov and Volgograd regions. In the first case, candidate Alexei Mitrofanov campaigned with the slogans "Criminal Southerners – out of the Pskov region!" In the second case, Alexei Golubyatnikov did the same with the slogan "This is not the Caucasus!" Both men were from the LDPR party. In both cases, representatives of local ethnic communities sent demands to the electoral committee to cancel the registration of the candidates for inciting ethnic hatred; both pleas were rejected. Two candidates to the State Duma from the 199th electoral region (Moscow) used nationalist slogans: Georgy Benyaguev (upset by the fact that a million Azerbaijanis lived in Moscow) [88]and Peotr Khomyakov (a former member of the National-Republican Party of Russia and the Congress of Russian Communities, now a member of the 'Rodina' Party).[89] A well-known national-radical, leader of the Party of Freedom (former National-Republican Party) Yuri Belyaev, was the latter's official assistant. In May 2004, a criminal case was thrown out against Belyaev due to the expiration of the statute of limitations.

Both the LDPR and Rodina actively used ethno-nationalist rhetoric. Both parties chanted slogans for the "defense of the Russian nation" and singled out the Russian people as the "state-forming nation" during the electoral campaign for President in 2004. We must note that *all* candidates for President used nationalist rhetoric to some extent, except Irina Khakamada (Vladimir Putin and Ivan Rybkin did not participate in the debates).[90]

---

86   "24 chasa" (24 Hours). *REN-TV,* 5/12/2004; Pushkar', Dmitry. "Piar na vechnykh izgnannikakh" (PR at eternal outcasts). *Moskovskie Novosti,* 24/12/2004 No. 49.

87   Vyugin, Mikhail. "Posledniy vrag" (Last Enemy). *Rossiya,* 5-11/8/2004. P. 8.

88   "A zachem Moskve million azerbaydzhantsev?" (Why are there a million Azerbaijanis in Moscow?). Interview with candidate for deputy in the State Duma in the 199th electoral region of Moscow Georgi Benyaguev. *Pravda* 199, 22/09/2004.

89   The elections of December 5th 2004 were called invalid.

90   More about the use of nationalist rhetoric during the presidential campaigns: Kozhevnikova, G. *Yazyk vrazhdy v predvybornoy agitatsii i vne ee"* (Hate Speech in Election Campaigns). Moscow: SOVA, 2004, pp. 92-103.

It is difficult to recognize or calculate the benefits of using nationalist rhetoric as a tool to win elections (in contrast to the previous election).[91] The presidential elections did not carry much intrigue. The pre-determined character of the presidential election didn't elicit much interest from the casual voter, leaving only specialists to analyze the actual campaigning. Nationalists in all other elections as usual did not achieve great success. Various experts attribute the success of the Rodina Party in the 2003 elections not to Rogozin and his nationalism, but to Glaziev and his social-populist ideas.[92]

However, the number of candidates using nationalist rhetoric grew immensely, revealing a huge electoral potential in the future for such a strategy.

---

91 More about electoral results of radical nationalists. "Natsional-patrioty, Tserkov' i Putin. Izbiratel'nye kampanii 1999 i 2000 gg" (National patriots, the Church and Putin. Electoral Campaigns 1999 and 2000). Moscow, 2000 (http://www.panorama. ru/works/patr/#elect).

92 Tselms, Georgy. "'Ya nenavizhu – znachit ya sushchestvuyu'. Gruppovoy portret ksenofoba v postsovetskom inter'ere" ('I hate – therefore, I exist' Group portraits of xenophobia in the post-Soviet region). *Russkiy Kur'er,* 17/12/2004 (http://www. ruskur.ru/text.php?identity=15789).

Conclusions

Looking back to the past year, we can conclude the following.

Firstly, in 2004, negative trends of the past persisted: spontaneous interethnic clashes; active use of nationalist slogans as an electoral resources; the denial by all level of government of the wide spread of nationalist sentiments and of the number of violent crimes motivated by nationalism; and the lack of political will in combating nationalist propaganda. We also observed an overall growth of xenophobic attitudes in Russian society, as well the rise of illegal activities by nationalist youth groups and organized political movements.

Secondly, new tendencies appeared in the activities of radical nationalist groups. Not only did they turn to violence more frequently, but they committed more murders too (mostly by knives). 2004 witnessed the political murder of Nikolai Girenko and other incidents when nationalist groups openly threatened anti-fascists or took responsibility for attacks. Nationalists were also able to organize propagandistic events at a national, large-scale level. In 2004, for the first time, representatives of respectable Russian parties, including those from United Russia, were seen openly supporting several nationalist events.

On the other hand, there were some positive developments in the counteractions to radical nationalism. In 2004 the Minister of Internal Affairs for the first time admitted the existence of skinheads in the country. A positive dynamic regarding the prosecution of nationalists started to take shape, mostly with respect to violent crimes. However, the resistance to nationalist manifestations by law enforcement authorities is still insufficient. Also new in 2004 was the emergence of spontaneous protests by potential victims, as well as the active self-defense, sometimes armed, against such nationalist attacks.

Appendix

Xenophobic Initiatives and the Media's Reaction to Them

If the use of nationalist rhetoric at the time of the presidential campaigns caused a fair amount of indignation in the press, then in the long run, the overall reaction to discriminatory initiatives gradually started to weaken.

The terrorist acts at the end of August and the beginning of September, especially the tragedy of Beslan, provoked a whole row of undertakings, which to a certain degree assisted the long-term growth of xenophobia in the country.

Two large-scale events of a similar kind occurred in September 2004. They were the proposals by Moscow State Duma Deputy Yuri Popov on re-strictions of the right to movement according to ethnicity (see above) and the toughening of migration legislature in the State Duma.

Popov's initiative in September evoked a common, negative response. The deputy has tried to pass his bill at least since 2000; however, up until September 2004, the bill has not attracted such close attention and caused a widespread, unequivocal effect in society. The range of negative reactions to the document was unexpectedly wide. The variety of responses included simple statements of the unconstitutionality of the bill, jokes on the site "Vladimir Vladimirovich[tm]"[93] and parallels to Nazi Germany. During the May discussion of the bill, chairman of the Moscow City Duma Vladimir Platonov strongly announced that he would do everything possible to ensure that the bill would never be passed: "It may be, will you insert the compass into law, as the fascists did? You know, they measured the circumference of the skull with compasses as well as the distance between the eyes, thus determining racial identity".[94] Platonov went on to strongly affirm his position practically with the same words. Sergei Buntman called the bill 'Nazi' during a program on *Echo of Moscow* radio dedicated to the bill. Practically all other partici-

---

93   Vladimir Vladimirovich (http://vladimir.vladimirovich.ru/2004-9-8/#an826).
94   "V Mosgordume obsudili nezvannykh gostey" (Moscow State Duma discusses unin-vited guests). *Kommersant*, 25/05/2004.

pants of the program joined that opinion – Andrei Khazin (senator from the Kostroma region) and Mark Urnov.[95] Even mayor Yuri Luzhkov in the wake of the scandal, who after each terrorist act insists on the legalization and toughening of the regime of registration in Moscow, hurried to dissociate himself from this initiative. Speaking at the conference "Diplomacy of Cities," he pledged to fight not with terrorism and migration, but with the reasons that spawn them.[96]

In contrast to this united negative response, only the newspaper *Komsomolskaya Pravda* managed not to cover the ethnic content of Popov's proposal. The newspaper was outraged by the uncontrollable migration, obviously pointing to migrants from the Caucasus region.[97]

The position of State Duma Chairman Boris Gryzlov was not completely clear. At the above-mentioned conference "Diplomacy of Cities," he stated that *"the modern city should save its face in spite of migration,"* but the *"strengthening of measures of safety and restriction of migration"* was needed *"under conditions of tolerance, under democratic principles, and within the framework of the Constitution.[98]"*

However, it is possible that this statement by the Chairman was not a reaction to Popov's bill, but a declaration of support for the "anti-terrorist group of laws," brought to discussion in the lower house in September. This group included bills toughening the migration legislature. Since the information about "antiterrorist initiatives" was extremely vague, there has never been a clear reaction to his words. We'd like to comment on that.

Firstly, the slightest hint at ethnically oriented bills, discussed in the State Duma, was subject to resistance, as was the bill by Popov. This, in particular, is related to the hint expressed in a statement by the chairman of the

---

95   *Ekho Moskvy,* 11/09/2004.

96   Voloshina, Victoria. "Zhizn' v Londone, Parizhe i Berline ne legche, chem v Moskve" (Life in London, Paris, and Berlin is not easier than in Moscow). *Izvestiya,* 17/09/2004.

97   Olifirova, Svetlana "V stolitsu ne khotyat puskat' inogorodnikh" (The capital does not want to let out-of-towners in). *Komsomolskaya Pravda,* 07/09/2004; Baranets, Viktor, Falaleev, Mikhail. "V chem my slabee terroristov" (How we are weaker than the terrorists). *Komsomolskaya Pravda,* 17/09/2004. P. 6-7.

Committee for Constitutional Legislation and State Structure Vladimir Pligin about the possibility of limiting the number of immigrants into *"regions with a complicated demographic and criminal environment."*[99] At any rate, the statement by Moscow region Governor Boris Gromov about the necessity of "examining registration" caused a singular negative response in the Moscow region, although the governor specially emphasized (this was conscientiously expressed by the journalists) that he had in mind not an administrative check according to ethnic traits, but a check of all migrants from the Caucasus.

Secondly, "anti-migrant" initiatives in the State Duma found a response in two conceptual articles, proving that migration under the current condition in Russia was a good thing. There were not similar reactions to the proposals by Popov; then the indignation had a completely emotional character. On the 18th of September, *Rossijskaya Gazeta* published a lengthy interview with the Ombudsman in the Russian Federation Vladimir Lukin.[100] On September 20th, an article by the chairman of the Executive Committee of "Forum of Migration Organizations" in *Izvestiya* was published.[101] In these articles, the modern migration legislation in Russia was considered absolutely Draconian. It is impossible to follow this law; therefore the majority of migrants are actually being forced out of the legal field. The further toughening of these laws will contribute only to the growth in the number of illegal immigrants and will definitely not assist the fight with terrorism. Meanwhile, in Russia, 'migrantophobia' is closely connected with 'ethnophobia'. Thus, the government on one hand refers to migrants as criminals comprising a potential terrorist threat, and on the other, removes migrants from legal jurisdiction. These approaches are contributing to the rise and wide spread of nationalist sentiments in Russia.

98   Voloshina, Victoria. "Zhizn' v Londone, Parizhe i Berline ne legche, chem v Moskve" (Life in London, Paris, and Berlin is not easier than in Moscow). *Izvestiya,* 17/09/2004.

99   Rodin, Ivan, Koriya, Anastasiya, Latuhina, Kira. "Terroristov budut 'mochit'" po mestu propiski: Zakonodateli planiruyut sushchestvenno ogranichit' pravo rossiyan na svobodu peredvizheniya" (Terrorists will be caught at the place of residence: Legilators plan to limit the right of Russians to free movement). *Nezavisimaya Gazeta,* 20/09/2004 (http://www.ng.ru/printed/politics/2004-09-20/1_propiska.html).

100   "Terrorist ne budet prosit' grazhdanstvo" (Terrorist will not ask for citizenship). *Rossijskya Gazeta,* 18/09/2004.

101   "Milliony v lovushke, ili ot kakikh nelegalov nado spasat' Rossiyu" (Millions in a trap, or we need to save Russia from illegals). *Izvestiya,* 20/09/2004.

Another event must be discussed here. On October 29th 2004, General Prosecutor of Russia Vladimir Ustinov presented a proposal of "reciprocal hostage takings," which caused a wide societal reaction and condemnation at an international level. However the statement by the prosecutor, in all its monstrosity, did not carry an ethnic tone, and its criticism did not touch upon it possible nationalist interpretation either. In September, when following the Beslan events, mass media outlets discussed the resumption of the Ossetian-Ingush conflict and the ethnic composition of terrorist groups, the motive of "reciprocal hostage takings" had already emerged. The first time this idea was brought up on September 3, 2004, when the newspaper *Izvestiya* published a whole block of materials (three articles on the topic and one letter from a reader), which focused on the possibility of using force against terrorist through their relatives. These measures were considered expedient, accept-able, and blameless, including those, which proposed the murder of relatives, and, as a rule, were thought to be in line with Chechen and Islamic tradi-tions.[102] These publications went practically unnoticed in the background of the scandal over the firing of the main editor of the newspaper Raf Shakirov, who was removed on September 5th. During those post-Beslan days, Dmitry Rogozin and Aman Tuleev called for the idea of collective responsibility for the terrorist attacks in the various newspapers.[103] Since both men had previ-ously spoken in the same style, their words attracted the attention of only pro-fessional commentators. As a whole, the topic of collective responsibility for terrorism did not attract much attention in September. However, it is clear that the statement in October by the General Prosecutor did not come out of no-where, but had support in many respectable political circles of Russia and is closely connected with nationalist ideas (it is indicative that on the wave of the

---

102   "Kak izbezhat' ksenofobii v moment natsional'nogo krizisa" (How to avoid xenopho-bia at the moment of a national crisis). Monitoring of press in the first week after Beslan".

103   Kostyakov, Anatoly. "Prishla pora vyvodit' bul'dozery" (The time has come to bring bulldozers). *Nezavisimaya Gazeta*, 13/09/2004 (http://www.ng.ru/printed/politics/ 2004-09-13/1_rogozin.html); Alekseev, Igor, Tuleev, Aman "Terrorizm – eto ab-solutnoe zlo i v bor'be s nim opravdony lyubye mery" (Terrorism is an absolute evil and in the fight with it, any measures are justified). *Nezavisimaya Gazeta*, 10/09/2004.

societal indignation against the initiative of the General Prosecutor, Dmitry Rogozin publicly condemned it).[104]

Since all of the discussed scandalous initiatives appeared in a relatively short period of time, criticism of them often carried a "complex" character – mostly surrounding the inability of the state to honorably solve the crisis situation, and the discussion of how to effectively minimize the consequences of the Beslan tragedy. Experts emphasized the necessity of overcoming ethnic stereotypes, fixing the intercultural dialogue, and the resolute struggle with manifestations of radical nationalism.[105] Most of all, from our point of view, Alexander Arkhangelski summed up the common negative reception to the officials' projects: *"To date, it has seemed as if the distinction between the crazy Chechen partisans and the regular Russian army is that behind the one stands a ringleader, controlling incomes, expenses, and corpses, and behind the other – the state, controlling the enforcement of the law. Controlling poorly, using double standards. But still forced to take the cases of Budanov and Ulman to trial. Now it turns out to be that the best solution to the root of terror will be the final destruction of the legal state, the regular army, and common moral, the final becoming like Maskhadov's and Basaev's riffraff."[106]*

In spite of the fact that proposals to take hostages voiced in September of 2004 went almost unnoticed, as a whole the reaction to xenophobic or potentially xenophobic initiatives by officials in September was strong and extremely negative. However, the stressful situation gradually began to pass into history and the reaction changed.

Thus, after the Moscow City Government tabled bills by Popov on October 13, Popov received unexpected support in public speeches by his colleague, the chairman of the City Government Committee for Economic Politics Irina Rukina. At the end of October at a press conference, and a month later (November 25) in an interview with *Komsomolskaya Pravda*, Rukina

---

104   "Mozno li borot'sya s terroristami ikh zhe metodami" (Can one fight terrorists using their own methods?). *Ekho Moskvy*, 0/11/2004.

105   Karaganov, Sergei. "Nuzhna modernizatsiya vsekh silovykh struktur" (Modernization of all power structures is needed). *Izvestiya*, 06/09/2004. Oreshkin, Dmitry. "Nado borot'sya ne za territorii, a za lyudey" (We need to fight not for territory, but for people). *Izvestiya*, 07/09/2004.

106   Arkhangelski, Alexandr. "Rubezh" (Border). *Izvestiya*, 13/09/2004 (http://www.izvestia.ru/comment/article372665).

openly supported the initiatives of Popov, referring to the fact that "*ethnic groups are seizing large sectors of the economy.*" These words by the Moscow Deputy are remarkable for a couple of reasons. Firstly, it was the first (and probably the only) appreciation of Popov's project by a non-marginal politician (Irina Rukina is a former member of the SPS, and a member of the Party of Life, headed by Mironov). Secondly, both of her supporting speeches were not met with any criticism. Thirdly, they were preceded by a quite fundamental (although probably mediated) ideological preparation. During a month, *Komsomolskaya Pravda* had published several very aggressive articles dedicated to migration, where the real social problem had been presented mainly as an ethnic problem having an obvious criminal component. It was a series of articles entitled "There are no more Russian children in kindergartens."

In November, *Komsomolskaya Pravda* also published another article which, from our point of view, certainly deserved a strong societal reaction, but which never came about.[107] Mikhail Yuriev wrote an article titled "The Internal Enemy and the National Idea." The overwhelming majority of the small number of reviews of this article was dedicated not to an analysis of the ideological points, which the ex-member of the Yabloko party tried to formulate in his article. Instead, these responses included declarations of implausibility of the author as a theorist, attempts to guess whom exactly the author identified as "enemies" or doubts in the mental health of the author.[108]

The ideological evaluation of Yurev's ideas, which he presented to the readers of *Komsomolskaya Pravda* (the most widely read newspaper in Russia), was made only a couple of times later. For example, these included the very unsuccessful (from our viewpoint) conversation between Eugenia Albats and M. Yurev on *Echo of Moscow* radio, where the host directly called the article a "manifestation of Russian fascism." Furthermore, during a program on the *Radio Liberty* Kirill Kobrin stated that any publication in which "enemies

---

107 We have in mind exactly the public reaction, since it was affirmed that the article was widely discussed in the "Live Journal" Brahman Ilya, "Vrag vnutri" (Enemy Inside). *Inache* (http://www.inache.net/barrikad/vragi.html).

108 See for example. Butrin, Dmitry. "Traktaty o vnutrennem vrage" (Treatises on the Internal Enemy). *Volgogradskaya Pravda*, 15/11/2004 (http://www.volgapravda. ru/articles/2004/11/15/1943/).

are identified and when it is said that Russia is a country for Russians," needs to be called chauvinistic, nationalist, extremely dangerous, and provocative. Maxim Sokolov in an article entitled "In the Struggle with Internal Ene-mies: New National-Ideological Experience," published on the web-site *GlobalRus* on November 12th, was able to make out a positive idea of Yurev, that was worthy of further discussion: *"It is dangerous not to have a moderate and responsible opposition, which is not full of splashed hatred for Russia and to which – in particular, thanks to the last quality – it would be possible to hand over power, not fearing terrible repercussions. If Yurev had developed this thought (which a friendly eye can, though with some difficulty, find in his article), he might have made a good thing, but, giving himself up to a violently intoxicating discussion of enemies, he ruined his entire song. If it was just a song of his own– then no big loss. But if this was not done just by him, but there was some other combination – then it means that another feeler is lost."*[109] Finally, in a conceptual discussion with Yurev in *Komsomolskaya Pravda*, Andrei Zabalishin[110] proved that Yurev writes based on principally incorrect representations of modern Russia, which makes all of his ideological ideas unconvincing.

It is probable that this refusal to hold a substantive discussion with Yurev was deliberate. That is already a reaction in itself. However, it is rather doubtful, whether such reaction is appropriate. One can boycott a similar arti-cle by the author printed in *Novaya Gazeta*, which has a completely deter-mined and ideologically formulated readership.[111] But can we ignore the "manifest," appearing on the pages of *Komsomolskaya Pravda*, which today has the highest readership, and more importantly is oriented at the most ideo-logically impressionable audience – teenagers?

In October 2004, another topic was clearly articulated for the first time – an ethnic ghetto for migrants – uttered by anonymous St. Petersburg busi-

---

109   Sokolov, M. "V bor'be s vnutrennim vragom" (In the fight with the internal enemy). *Globalrus.ru,* 12/11/2004 (http://www.globalrus.ru/opinions/138899).

110   Zabalisin, Andrei "Zachem Rossiyu dolzhen boyat'sya mir?" (Why should the world be afraid of Russia?). *Komsomolskaya Pravda,* 2/12/2004. [Taken from the site: Na-tions of Russia. Unity and Diversity: http://www.narodru.ru/smi361.html].

111   Yur'ev, Mikhail. "Krepost' Rossiya" (The fortress of Russia). *Novaya Gazeta,* 17/05/2004 (http://2004.novayagazeta.ru/nomer/2004/17n/n17n-s44.shtml).

nessmen (see above). The conversation did not revolve around illegal immigrants, but about people legally working in Russia. A review of the roundtable was published in *Rosbalt* information agency and did not attract *any* attention. Another initiative of the St. Petersburg officials also went unnoticed: as "an effort to provide safety for foreign students", it was proposed to concentrate the students in one place and then guarantee their safety there. However, that is impossible to interpret as anything other than the recognition of the lack of power of the Petersburg government.

Neither television channels nor the press put forth clear criticism of these initiatives. Only once, on the eve of the International Day of Migration, did the *Rossiyskaya Gazeta* publish a review of the meeting with journalists by the deputy director of the Federal Migration Service (FMS) of Russia Igor Yunash and an official of Russian Academy of Science working on problems of migration Irina Malakha. At the meeting, in particular, a question was posed on the participants' relationship to the idea of "special housing for guest workers." Malakha clearly spoke against the idea, while the deputy of the FMS did not offer a clear position. However, during the press conference, it was he who publicly offered advice on how to circumvent present migration laws: to receive a migration card, *"a person should if only for a minute cross our border. It doesn't matter where. Exit somewhere, let's say, at the Ukrainian border, go for a walk there and then go up to a border point. A few act differently: they arrive at the airport, buy a ticket, pass to the safe zone, then refuse to fly, return, and receive a migration card.* Formally, we need to bring formal changes to the law, but this is quite complicated." [emphasis mine – G.K.][112]

More criticism for such initiatives rarely appeared in the printed mass media. Even Andrei Kolesnikov, who is regularly published in the *Rossijskaya Gazeta* criticizing "state xenophobia," published his article about the migration camps only on the portal Gazeta.ru.

At the same time, the Kuban government came up with the idea of the creation of "filtration camps" for illegal migrants (see above). The administra-

---

112   Smolyakova, Tat'yana. "Granitsy peresekli lyudey" (Borders have intersected with people). *Rossiyskaya Gazeta,* 18/12/2004 (http://www.rg.ru/2004/12/18/migranty. html).

tion of the region, recognizing the doubtful legality of the project, has constantly appealed to the regional prosecutor, which has confirmed the authorization for the creation of the camps. The initiative has been covered not only in the local press. In particular, the opening of the camps was reported in one of the news segments on TV-Tsentr, which has the status of a national channel. There the initiative was presented as a positive example of the fight against illegal migration.

Surprisingly, in comparison with the relatively active polemics on the problems of migration, discussions of the problems surrounding the "ghetto" or "deportations" are practically non-existent.

Thus, in the month following the Beslan events, when the negative responses to even potentially xenophobic initiatives were sufficiently strong, the subsequent reaction in the later months to similar proposals dwindled to zero. However, the theme of xenophobia has never disappeared completely from the pages of newspapers. Most often the issue is raised in relation to the question of migration. Experts, standing by its necessity and not denying a whole range of problems, are trying to objectively look at all related questions – economic, cultural, social, etc. By the way, discussions on migration have most precisely shown the evolution of the "hate speech" in the Russian mass media. In the rhetoric of those against migration (both politicians and journalists) the nationalist "hate speech" is gradually being closely woven together with the social "hate speech," where accusations against ethnicities are being forced out by accusations against migrants or even mixed with them. However, the subject of migration is the only "living" problem of the ones being discussed having a xenophobic overtone. As in past, the most apparent reverberations in society are being reported (for example, the practically justified sentence of Victor Korchargin). Commentaries by experts and rights defenders appear, but in general they only appear as statements of the growth of xenophobia in Russian society and criticisms of government policy as one of the reasons for this growth.

The debate of ways to counteract the prevalence of nationalist sentiments is gradually being reduced. It was particularly obvious during the "active" September background. It is completely possible that elements of censure have been at play here. However, statements against xenophobia (migrantophobia, ethnophobia) became commonplace, just as did the repeated accusations directed at the government. There is nothing new in this, and nothing new to discuss. It is possible that one of the reasons for this is that attention to this topic by society fell and as a result, positive articles that discussed the issue in the papers also disappeared.

II. The 2005 Annual Report

1. Introduction

This review covers key manifestations of radical ethno-nationalism in Russia, and opposition to it by society and the state in 2005. As before, it is based on daily monitoring by SOVA Center[1]; all materials used in this review, except when indicated otherwise, can be found on the Center's Nationalism and Xenophobia website: http://xeno.sova-center.ru.

The past year was marked by more than just the further development of past (alarming, but not unusual) right-wing radical trends. These include the growth of racist and other hate-motivated violence, increasingly aggressive day-to-day xenophobia, and exploitation of ethno-nationalist sentiments in elections. The year 2005 also witnessed some new tendencies concerning right-wing radicalism, which were underestimated by the state and could potentially lead to serious consequences.

2. Manifestations of Radical Nationalism

2.1. Violence

Similarly to previous years, hate-motivated violence in Russia was mainly associated with skinheads. Their attacks became more frequent, while slightly less cruel (in 2005, 18 fewer people were killed than in 2004). Moreover, whereas in previous years we could identify more or less clear-cut "groups at risk" targeted by skinheads, such as people with dark skin or peo-

---

1   See last year's report: Kozhevnikova G. "Radikal'nyy natsionalizm v Rossii: proyavleniya i protivodeystvie" (Radical nationalism in Russia: Manifestations and Responses). *Natsionalizm i ksenofobiya*. SOVA Center, 24 January 2005 (http://xeno.sova-center.ru/29481C8/4DCF65B). SOVA Center's activities are presented at http://sova-center.ru.

ple from Central Asia, now it is increasingly difficult to determine which groups skinheads are likely to attack. Today victims do not need to be Azeri or Chinese; having slightly darker skin or hair, or just "turning up at the wrong moment" makes one vulnerable. Skinheads are increasingly likely to attack members of youth subcultures believed by skinheads to be "traitors of the white race" - rappers, punks, skaters, Goths, and others, as well as the ideological opponents of the skinhead movement, the leftist anti-fascist youth.[2] In addition, we should note that while in 2004 skinhead groups claimed responsibility for racist attacks only in a few cases, in 2005 they did so consistently.

Table 1:   Comparative statistics of victims of racist and neo-Nazi attacks in 2004-2005

YEAR	2004		2005	
TOTAL	KILLED	BEATEN, INJURED	KILLED	BEATEN, INJURED
	49	218	47	418
INCLUDING				
Dark-skinned people	1	33	3	38
People from Central Asia	9	23	16	34
People from the Caucasus	15	38	12	52
People from the Middle East and North Africa	4	12	1	22
People from Asia-Pacific Region (China, Viet-Nam, Mongolia, etc.)	8	29	4	58
Other people of "non-Slav appearance"	2	22	3	72
Members of youth subcultures and leftist youth	0	4	3	121
Others, or not known	10	57	5	21

---

2   Strictly speaking, we should differentiate between "red skinheads" that include some of young anti-fascists, and Nazi skinheads - their opponents. But we will follow the tradition and use the term 'skinhead' to describe Nazi skinheads and "boneheads" and will not use the term with regard to their opponents.

As before, these statistics do not include homeless people and victims of robbery and other property offences, unless the hate motive in such crimes is specifically recognized by law enforcement agents. For example, we did not include the attack against a Rwandan in Voronezh or the killing of an Azeri man in Nizhniy Novgorod in a fight provoked by offensive nationalist behavior, in which the perpetrators stole the victim's car. We also did not include victims of skinheads' "revenge" attacks against their former members, and victims of massive fights, in which the number of people affected is difficult to assess. So our statistics are, by design, underestimated, but reliable to the maximum extent possible without a detailed study of each specific case.

We should note that between 2004 and 2005, mass media policies changed with regard to covering this type of offences. In an increasing number of cases, racist attacks were covered many months after the incident, when the crime had been already investigated and the perpetrator convicted. It created a false impression of high detection rates for such offences, and an illusion that most skinheads involved in violent racist offences were eventually punished. But this was not true.

Still, even though the media coverage of such attacks was far from complete, and given the restrictive standards we use to determine racist motives, it is obvious that the number of victims is rapidly growing: the recent statistics exceed those of the previous year by more than 1.5 times, even by very conservative estimates.

Skinhead attacks have become so common that they are no longer perceived as "news," but as part of everyday life. For this type of crime to be noticed it must be either designed to elicit public response (as the killing of anti-fascist musician Timur Kacharava in St. Petersburg on 13 October 2005) or result in spontaneous protests which cannot be ignored (as in October 2005 in Voronezh, following the killing of a student from Peru, or in St. Petersburg after the killings of African students).

While Moscow (16 people killed, 179 injured) and St. Petersburg (4 killed, 45 injured) remained the epicenters of racist violence, the geographic distribution of such violence is consistently spreading. While in 2004 we documented attacks in 26 regions, in 2005 they were reported in 36 regions. In addition to Russian and NIS nationals, people from at least 25 countries were victimized in 2005.

Good news: fewer killings. The difference in numbers is so significant that it cannot be explained only by different policies of media coverage. We can assume that it may have been caused by increased sentencing for killings, put forth by policies enacted since 2004 (see below).[3]

While skinheads were the perpetrators of racist attacks in most Russian regions, in South Russia[4] racist violence was primarily associated with Cossacks. However, in 2005, Cossacks began to see skinheads as "comrades-in-arms." It is obvious since the Movement against Illegal Immigration became active in southern regions of Russia; the movement openly recruits skinheads to its ranks. Such collaboration was displayed through an incident in Novorossiysk, in which during a trial of a skinhead who attacked a Roma man, leaflets were distributed with appeals *"not to let them convict a young Cossack."* Moreover, representatives of right-wing radical organizations closely linked to skinheads – Dmitry Dyomushkin of the Slavic Union and Alexander Ivanov (Sukharevsky) of the Popular National Party - openly and formally attended the All-Russian Cossack Circle, a congress held on 10 July outside Kursk.[5]

Cossacks were involved in the three biggest ethnic clashes reported in Russia in 2005. In March in Novorossiysk, a street fight between Cossacks and young Armenians and Greeks resulted in an anti-Armenian pogrom. On the day following the street fight 22 March, Cossacks raided and destroyed a cafe owned by an ethnic Armenian and demolished a few cars. The city authorities had to mobilize all law enforcement units to stop Cossacks coming

---

3   The figures have changed substantially since the time when the original report was written. Hence, a real reduction in the murder statistics did not occur. But they did not exceed the level of the last year either, which is a positive factor compared to the subsequent development.

4   In this paper, we cannot cover the situation in the North Caucasus republics. The events there should be the subject of a different type of research. The data available for Dagestan, Kabardino-Balkaria and especially Chechnya cannot be treated in the same way as the data for Stavropol and Krasnodar. Therefore, our statistics do not include these republics, and we use the term "the Russian South" to include regions, which are part of the Southern Federal District, minus the above-mentioned republics.

5   At the congress, Demushkin and Ivanov (Sukharevsky) - long-term competitors accusing each other of collaboration with Russian security agencies - even had a physical fight "for leadership."

from outside of the city and from neighboring settlements and in order to prevent even more violence. The atmosphere in the city was tense for weeks afterwards, with Cossacks disseminating leaflets calling for pogroms and threatening to block the federal highway.

Russian media widely covered the anti-Chechen riots in the village of Yandyki outside Astrakhan in August. The violence was provoked by a fairly mild sentence given to three ethnic Chechens convicted for hate-motivated vandalism in a rural cemetery and a street fight killing a local villager – an ethnic Kalmyk. His funeral resulted in attacks against Chechens and arson attacks against their homes; the attackers included, in addition to local residents, Kalmyks and Cossacks who came from neighboring districts and from Kalmykia.

As a result of the clashes, at least five people were hospitalized (by unofficial data, at least 30 were hospitalized, and the overall number of victims is unknown), and at least five houses of the Chechen families were burnt to ashes. To stop the riots, a village of about three thousand inhabitants had to be sealed off by more than a thousand police and interior forces brought in from neighboring regions. The administrative border with Kalmykia had to be completely closed.

Also in August, another heated situation almost erupted in a riot against ethnic Chechens in Rostov region, where an ethnic Chechen was accused of raping the daughter of a Cossack leader. The local Cossacks announced "mobilization" and brought more than four hundred men to the village. Police succeeded in curbing the riots, but the Cossack camps surrounded the village for several more days.

The three conflicts described above demonstrated the rapid deployment ability of Cossack units and their high readiness for violent action. Moreover, Cossacks have openly made it clear that they were prepared to assume law enforcement functions – in accordance with their own understanding of the law.

The right-wing radicals have been increasingly explicit in their demonstrations of readiness for political terrorism. They go beyond threats against top-ranking officials[6] and openly engage in violence. In 2005 two high-profile incidents were suspected of being orchestrated by radical nationalists.

On March 17, 2005, in an assassination attempt, Anatoly Chubais's motorcade was raked with automatic weapons fire. On suspicion of organizing and committing the assault, Colonel Vladimir Kvachkov, a member of the Military Imperial Union, was arrested, and Ivan Mironov, the son of ex-cochairman of the National Imperial Party Boris Mironov, was declared wanted (the son, like the father, is a right-wing radical activist).

On 12 June, an attempted blast attack on a passenger train heading from Grozny to Moscow, fortunately, did not cause deaths or serious injuries. Two activists of ethno-nationalist groups were charged with organization of the attack.

There are serious reasons to suspect right-wing radicals to have been involved in the pressure on the participants of the so-called Blokhin-Konovalenko trial. Back in 2003, these two policemen from the city of Dolgoprudny outside Moscow were charged with abuse of power in detaining a local criminal leader who was ethnically from the Caucasus. The criminal leader was released on recognizing the mistake, disappeared and is currently on the federal list of wanted suspects. It would have remained just another case of police abuse if the local right-wing radicals had not interfered. In 2004, two judges and a prosecutor involved in the proceedings were attacked separately, with one judge being killed. The local chapter of the Russian National Unity (RNE) claimed responsibility for the three incidents, and proclaimed itself to be a "support group for Russian police." Then the proceedings were transferred to Moscow, but the threats continued, targeting virtually all participants of the trial. In summer 2005, a jury court acquitted the defendants, but in September, the Russian Supreme Court overruled the judgment by formally recognizing that members of the jury had been pressured into passing a non-guilty verdict (the fact that RNE was behind the pressure was informally admitted even by the defendants' supporters). Whatever the real motives of RNE (known for its close links with the criminal world), these actions were presented as protection of "Russian policemen" against the "Caucasian mafia." The case was sent back for re-consideration, and a new criminal investi-

---

6   For example, the governor of St. Petersburg Valentina Matviyenko.

gation launched into the threats. Around the 20th of December, the wife of another trial participant was attacked.

As another sign of increasing readiness for terrorist acts, a number of ethno-nationalist organizations attempted the legal (or illegal[7]) acquisition of weapons and the creation of mobile armed units. In 2005, organizers of the All-Russian Officers' Assembly, the Slavic Union, and the RNE all called for such initiatives. However, the biggest response emerged as a result of the Movement against Illegal Immigration's call on Hitler's birthday on April 20, which was supported by MP Nikolai Kuryanovich of the Liberal-Democratic Party.

Growing xenophobia in Russian society (a survey by the Levada Center in summer found unprecedented rates of xenophobia in Russia) increasingly provoked racist violence by persons having nothing to do with right-wing radical groups. The most outrageous of reported incidents happened in Irkutsk region, where on 10 June local villagers in Moskovschina lynched Uzbek migrant workers for "being ethnically non-Russian" and looking similar to the previous team of workers suspected by locals of being involved in the deaths of several villagers. Two people were killed in the attack, and four more hospitalized with serious injuries. The head of the local administration, Sergey Zubarev, virtually justified the lynching by saying that the conflict had been provoked by the local businessman who should have stopped "bringing foreign workers to Moskovschina" and adding that "we, [ethnic] Russian people, are tolerant, but you should not test our tolerance for too long."[8] Sadly, even this outrageous incident was not totally new: a similar one happened in 2004 in Novosibirsk region, when about a dozen migrant workers from Azerbaijan were cruelly beaten for no reason, and about a hundred (!) local residents came to watch the beating.

The incident in Moskovschina in 2005, being the cruelest, was just one of many similar incidents. Xenophobic violence by non-affiliated Russians was reported in Samara, Pskov, and Sverdlovsk regions.

Notably, in 2005, for the first time law enforcement authorities recognized the ethnic hatred motive in an incident involving the use of firearms

---

7   The RNE is banned for illegal possession of weapons.
8   Migrant construction workers lynched in Moscovia. *Baykal Info*, 16 June 2005.

against a man from the Caucasus in Nizhniy Tagil; the attackers, apparently, were not affiliated with any right-wing radical groups.

A new phenomenon emerged in 2005. Skinhead violence and racist attacks were so common and potential victims were so intimidated that ordinary criminals increasingly took advantage of their fear by pretending to be neo-Nazis. Thus in 2005, street robbers "looking like skinheads" were arrested in Moscow and in Yekaterinburg. The offender detained in Moscow later explained to the police that the mimicry discouraged his victims from any resistance should he threaten that "the other guys" were coming to his help. In October in Irkutsk, killers attempted to mislead the investigation by painting a swastika on the wall next to the corpse.

2.2. Key areas of Activity of Organized Right-Wing Radical Groups

While early in the decade skinhead gang violence was the most obvious indicator of right-wing radical trends in Russia, in 2005 the focus on ideology became more prominent in right-wing radical groups. Alongside their old communication channels – such as rallies, newspapers, magazines, and websites - they increasingly use new, sometimes fairly unusual promotion tactics. We can even assume that they use strategic planning approaches to organize their promotion.

RNE may be the only group still keeping within the limits of "traditional" methods. It became notably active back in 2004 and maintained virtually the same pace in 2005. As before, RNE activists held a few pickets and disseminated leaflets calling for political terrorism. In early 2005, the part of RNE headed by Alexander Barkashov launched a new project under a trendy (then) title "*Pora!*" (It's high time!), but it never achieved popularity. In general RNE remains in a crisis, as its split parts continue fighting and accusing each other of collaboration with security services, etc. The impression of increased RNE activity is due, partially, to the overall atomization of right-wing radicals and partially to scandals involving members of the group. Such scandals include a massive fight with police on 9 May, provoked, apparently, by RNE members themselves; an attack by Barkashov and others on a policeman; and the conviction of a local RNE leader in Kareliya for murder in June 2005.

Right-wing radicals have long been concerned about the low resonance of antisemitic propaganda; the public has been more responsive to other ethnic phobias. Antisemitism has been traditionally the most prominent part of Russian nationalist propaganda.[9] Growing social discontent and fear of immigrants in Russia have forced nationalists to rethink their rhetoric. Most attempts have not been successful so far; for example, a meeting in Moscow adopted a resolution where alongside demands to raise salaries of health care workers and teachers, a call was made to investigate a ritual killing of five children by Hassids in Krasnoyarsk.[10]

The use of "social justice" slogans (notably, not just in January and February - at the time of massive protests against the "monetization of benefits" law - but throughout the year), coupled with traditional antisemitic propaganda, substantially expanded the audience reached by radical nationalists. The Movement against Illegal Immigration (DPNI) spread its propaganda more successfully than others not only by abandoning antisemitic references, but also by translating ethnic xenophobia into a more socially acceptable rejection of "immigrants," commonly understood as "ethnic aliens" from the South and the East in "traditionally ethnic Russian" areas.

Appeals to strong anti-immigrant sentiments in society, combined with active and radical propagandizing helped DPNI to become a leader - if not *the* leader – among right-wing radicals. Its power lies not in the relatively small core of active members, but in the mass of supporters, including respectable politicians and journalists. By the end of the year the leader of the movement, Alexander Potkin, who assumed the pseudonym Belov,[11] became the most

---

9   See the section on antisemitism. Radical Russian nationalists attempted to avoid antisemitism before. Such attempts were described in 2002 by A. Verkhovsky in his report "Russian nationalists are evading antisemitism." The report in Russian is available from SOVA Center website: http://xeno.sova-center.ru/1ED6E3B/ 1ED7483/215FBBA.

10   To remind the reader: five boys aged 10 – 11 disappeared in Krasnoyarsk in April 2005. After a long time, their bodies were found in an underground sewage reservoir in the city.

11   Alexander Sevast'yanov made the following statement about it: "For tactical reasons, the DNPI leadership gave him a party pseudonym: Belov, consistent with the country's revolutionary tradition (Stalin, Molotov, and many others)." However, rather than revolutionary, we see a racist tradition here ("Belov" comes from "bely" – "white" in Russian).

popular spokesman of Russian ethno-nationalists, beating the less charis-
matic Alexander Sevast'yanov. Potkin's professionalism in the field of public
relations came as a result of his previous work as press secretary for the
leader of Pamyat National Patriotic Front. Furthermore, as a talented dema-
gogue, he is almost always very careful with his rhetoric, making it difficult to
challenge his statements or to sue him for incitement to ethnic hatred.

Another strategic area of activity for right-wing radicals is the further integration of their ranks. There have been a few attempts to do so at events in
Altai,[12] Penza, Bryanks, Vladimir, and in the Far East. Notably, the establishment of the Russian Club in Vladivostok was not only an attempt at integration, but possibly, helped the Vladivostok neo-Nazis through a crisis caused
by a local "skinhead case".[13] It was followed by a number of nation-wide integration events.

In October, the Moscow chapter of the interregional non-governmental
movement "Russia's National Imperial Path" was registered; in fact, it was a
reincarnation of the National Imperial Party (NDPR), which was denied registration in 2003 under an atmosphere of a public scandal, but remained active
anyway. Back in 2002, NDPR was registered as a party and became a center
of integration that brought together a multitude of dwarfish or split right-wing
radical groups. On 3 December 2005, in Moscow, the National Imperial Path
– the reincarnated NDPR - held its periodic party convention and publicly
stated that by the spring of 2006 it planned to register the required number of
regional chapters in order to transform the movement into a political party,
and hence, be able to participate in the 2007 elections. This, however, seems
to be a long shot at the moment.

On 21 November, in Moscow, a "rehabilitation" congress of the Union of
Russian People was held to coincide with the 100th anniversary of the organization by the same name, but better known as The Black Hundred. The congress was attended by about 70 organizations of Orthodox Christian and
monarchist orientation. It was the first attempt in a few years to build a broad

---

12   At the end of 2004.
13   In 2004 in Vladivostok, a group of skinheads were detained on charges of several
      racist attacks. Ultimately, only one of them was convicted, but the others willingly
      testified against him. This incident strongly affected the morale of Vladivostok neo-
      Nazis.

coalition of ethno-nationalist monarchist organizations. The congress did not end up as just another marginal event; on the contrary, guest speakers included MP Sergey Glazyev, leader of (Rogozin's) Rodina parliamentary party, MP Sergey Baburin, Vice Speaker of the State Duma (of the other Rodina Party), and MP Nikolai Kuryanovich of the LDPR. Baburin officially joined the organization, headed by sculptor Vyacheslav Klykov.

The third strategic area of activity for right-wing radicals – traditional, rather than new, but increasing in intensity in 2005 – was "fighting for young people," in particular for skinheads. In fact, following the Orange Revolution in Ukraine, "fighting for young people" became a priority for virtually all stakeholders, ranging from the President's Administration that established the *Nashi* youth movement, to liberal political parties. Right-wing radicals followed along with the trend.

An entirely new project – the Eurasia Youth Union (ESM) – was launched in the spring of 2005 in the form of "fighting units" of the Eurasia Movement headed by Alexander Dugin, who as leader successfully combines his status of semi-official political advisor with the reputation of the leading ideologist of "Russian fascism".[14] ESM positions itself as an alternative to the commercialized and ideologically amorphous *Nashi*, emphasizes loyalty to the current government, and promotes the slogans of "opposing the Orange threat." ESM has already attracted public attention with a number of provocative acts, such as an attack on the Pentecostals' picket in Moscow,[15] attempts to disrupt oppositional events in the regions (Moscow, Bashkortostan, Krasnodar Territory), and their formal leading role during the November 2005 "Right-wing March" in Moscow.

They continue their efforts to win the support of young people. Thus, in Vladimir region, a boot camp organized by the Russian All-Nation Union ran throughout the summer of 2005. NDPR placed a special emphasis on young people as its key target group in all program documents. In fact, NDPR has been more active than all others in recruiting young people. One of NDPR leaders, Alexander Sevastyanov, spoke many times throughout the year to

---

14   See details, for example, in: Laruelle M. "Aleksandr Dugin kak ideologicheskiy posrednik" (Alexander Dugin is an ideological intermediary) in *Tsena nenavisti*. Moscow: SOVA Center, 2005, pp. 226–253.

young audiences in undergraduate schools, including reputable public univer-sities as well as private "commercial" ones.

Besides, NDPR made another attempt to get inside general schools. Building on its 2004 experience,[16] the NDPR chapter in Tomsk organized an essay contest for school students; the suggested theme was "What does be-ing [ethnic] Russian mean in Russia?" How they succeeded in involving schools in a contest held under a logo closely resembling a Nazi swastika is a mystery.

Some details of the "government-sponsored" efforts to "involve" skin-heads will follow below.[17] With regards to right-wing radicals collaborating publicly, before 2005, with rare exceptions,18 they were cautious about work-ing with neo-Nazi skinhead groups. Apparently, they perceived skinheads as an unmanageable, undisciplined mob. However, 2005 was a turning point in this respect as well. Even though we can dismiss the statements made in the spring by the right-wing radicals Yuri Belov and Yuri Riverov about involving skinheads in the White Patrol group[19] as mere self-promotion, there is no way we can ignore the involvement of skinheads in the "Right-wing March," which was organized in Moscow on 4 November 2005 by a coalition of right-wing radical organizations.[20]

The "Right-wing March" came as a logical consequence of the new offi-cial holiday established in 2005 – the Day of National Unity on 4 November. Everyone with at least some knowledge of Russian history found the idea of the new holiday questionable to say the least. The Right-wing March appar-ently had been planned as an event of national scale, or at least involving more than one region. However, in St. Petersburg the number of participants was traditionally low, no more than 150, while in Syktyvkar the local authori-

---

15   See below.
16   In 2003 – 2004, NDPR organized a similar competition on a national scale. See de-tails in: Kozhevnikova G. "Radikal'nyy natsionalizm v Rossii: proyavleniya i protivod-eystvie" (Radical nationalism in Russia: Manifestations and Responses). *Obzor sobytiy 2004 goda.*
17   See section Radical nationalism on behalf of the state.
18   Yu. Belyaev's Freedom Party, both People's National Parties - Tokmakov's and Ivanov's (Sukharevsky), and Dmitry Dyomushkin's Slavic Union.
19   Soon they were confused and could not make sense of their own information.

ties banned the march. But even the march held in Moscow produced enough impact, when about 3,000 people (mostly skinheads) walked the streets of the Russian capital carrying xenophobic, racist and explicitly neo-Nazi slogans. They completed the show by raising their arms in the Nazi salute.

The number of skinheads and the degree of discipline they showed during the march[21] suggested that legally operating organizations have broad and close links with neo-Nazi skinhead groups. These organizations also succeeded in managing the skinhead mob – at least for a short while – something that had been doubted both by experts and by the organizers of the march. There is no doubt now that all active right-wing radicals will increase their efforts to involve skinheads.

In addition to exploiting 'social justice' rallies to promote their ideologies, picketing court buildings during trials emerged as a new and effective promotional strategy for right-wing groups. Rather than campaigning for only those whom nationalist "patriots" consider their allies (such as members of Schults-88 group in St. Petersburg or RNE in Oryol), right-wing radicals preferred to focus on defendants victims of trials having nothing to do with nationalist ideology, but instead involving "[ethnic] Russians" vs. "members of other ethnicities/immigrants". Right-wing radicals appealed to the general public by interpreting such trials in terms of an interethnic confrontation. High-profile cases of this type included the trial of two policemen from Dolgoprudnyy (see above) and the Alexandra Ivannikova case (the woman, a Moscow resident, was charged with killing a man who attempted to rape her; the man was an ethnic Armenian).

Another effective form of self-promotion practiced in particular by the Slavic Union was website hacking. While before there had been only a few isolated cases of website hacking, in 2005 this activity became more targeted and consistent, especially after the hacker attacks against the websites of the Moscow Helsinki Group and the Federation of Jewish Communities in Russia (Jewish.ru), widely covered by mass media. For some reason, law enforce-

---

20   The actual organizers of the march included ESM, DPNI, and NDPR. Formally, ESM applied for permission to hold the march.

21   They refrained from fighting when a small group of anti-fascists started throwing water-filled condoms at them. There were not enough police around to stop a fight, should it have started.

ment authorities have been unable to suppress such offences, while the Slavic Union openly invites more hacker attacks as a *"good result* (apparently, meaning "method" – Author) *for breaking the information blockade."*

In 2005, another alarming trend emerged. Increasingly, we hear about joint events held by both right-wing and left-wing radicals, and even liberally oriented organizations. There is some evidence of collaboration between the Vanguard of Red Youth (AKM) and RNE in the city of Ramenskoye outside Moscow, and in Rostov-on-the-Don, while a joint picket in defense of RNE activists in Novgorod involved members of regional chapters of the National Bolshevik Party (NBP), Freedom Party, and, surprisingly, Yabloko Party. A rally in Moscow carrying ethno-nationalist slogans involved, alongside DPNI and NNP, activists of the Union of Communist Youth (SKM), Yabloko youth branch, etc. There have been even more examples of collaboration between seemingly democratic organizations and the Rodina Party.

2.3. Anti-Roma Attacks

Anti-Roma attacks were prominent in 2005. These were caused both by common (sometimes extremely absurd) xenophobic attitudes and also by targeted anti-Roma propaganda.

Thus, in the spring of 2005, city authorities in Krasnoyarsk were forced to deport all Roma rapidly from the city in order to prevent massive pogroms against them. The threat of riots was very real due to rumors that Roma were responsible for the disappearance of five school students.[22] Such actions by authorities were not the best (and, apparently, illegal) solution, but it appeared as if the city could not protect Roma in any other way.

Attacks against Roma were reported in Leningrad, Pskov, Moscow[23] and Belgorod regions. In Belgorod, the attack was professionally planned and organized: the road leading to the house was blocked, ostensibly, for repairs. The masked attackers first threw a bottle filled with flammable liquid at the house, and then started beating people fleeing the burning building, while

---

22 It was not known at the time that the children had died.
23 A group of local skinheads claimed responsibility for a riot of a Roma camp outside Moscow, injuring at least four.

shouting "Beat the Gypsies!" The woman who owned the house and her son had to be hospitalized, and it was only by chance that greater damage was avoided. The residents of the house were entertaining guests on that day, who were not only able to drive the attackers away, but even physically apprehend of them.

The biggest conflicts, however, first started back in 2004, and continued into 2005.

Mass media outlets have covered events around the Roma settlement in Iskitim, Novosibirsk region, on many occasions. They began in December 2004, when several houses of Roma residents were burned down under the pretext of fighting drug crimes. The arsons were apparently committed by local bandits, but were actively supported by other (non-Roma) residents and virtually encouraged by the police (by some reports, police would not allow either the fire brigades or ambulances to the sites of the arsons). Two more waves of arsons came in April and November, accompanied by intense anti-Roma campaigns in the local media (some local papers even suggested that Roma themselves burned down their houses, and that these people were linked with Chechen terrorists). For a long time police refused to respond to the events in any way; an investigation into the arson attacks was launched only after a parliamentary enquiry by the deputy head of the State Duma Committee on Civil, Criminal, Commercial and Procedural Legislation, Pyotr Shelisch from United Russia. He sent his enquiry to the Department of Interior of Novosibirsk in March 2005, and was immediately accused of corruption by the Novosibirsk press. Similarly, human rights groups that tried to help the victims were accused of aiding the drug dealers.

After a third wave of arson attacks in November 2005, when an eight-year-old girl was killed and her mother seriously injured by a bottle of inflammable liquid hitting her bed, a representative of the local prosecutor's office publicly stated that those responsible for the arson had been identified. However, these suspects did not face punishment, because the local public in Iskitim was worried about the spread of drugs in the region and wanted all Roma to move away. This statement suggests that the conflict in Iskitim is far from finished and will continue, encouraged by the local law enforcement authorities.

A similar scenario nearly took place in Yaroslavl region starting in November 2004, when Sergey Krivnyuk, deputy of the local municipality, said that he was prepared personally to lead riots against Roma on the pretext of fighting crime. Public statements by local drug police officials denying the culpability of Roma in drug trafficking helped to stem anti-Roma sentiments, and thus the threat of riots. These officials also raised the possibility of bringing criminal charges against the deputy.[24] Following the Iskitim events in the spring of 2005, S. Krivnyuk set up what he called "a community squad named after Che Guevara", which then demolished a few cars owned by Roma (there were no reports of victims). But as soon as Krivnyuk declared his involvement in organizing the "Che Guevara squad," the local police department started an inquiry into his conduct with a very real prospect of criminal prosecution. Notably, the mass media in Yaroslavl supported the law enforcement authorities by explaining to the local public why Krivnuyk's statements were dangerous.[25]

Yaroslavl region was one of the rare examples of an immediate and publicized response by law enforcement to such statements and actions. In contrast, in Irkutsk region, calls to anti-Roma riots voiced by Yevgeny Roizman,[26] MP of the State Duma and informal leader of the City without Drugs Fund in Yekaterinburg, were not opposed, but instead widely promoted by the local media.

In comparison to the atmosphere described above, the long-term conflict between a Roma community and the Mayor of Archangelsk over land plots allocated for construction of Roma houses looks fairly "civilized." The litigation lasted for more than 18 months and was finally won by the Mayor's office.[27] By the spring of 2006, all Roma houses were to be razed. During the

---

24   Later, unconfirmed reports appeared that a criminal investigation was opened into Krivnyk's statement under article 282 of the Criminal Code.

25   See, e.g. Oleg Kozlovsky. "Prezhde chem zhech' doma i vyselyt' tsygan." (Before you burn houses and evict Gypsies). *Golden Ring* (Yaroslavl'), 22 January 2005 (ht tp://www.goldring.ru/podrobno.php?id_rub=15798&day=22&month=1&year=2005).

26   The Fund is known for its anti-Roma and anti-Tajik statements, kidnapping drug addicts for the purpose of their treatment without medications (!) Royzman himself is known to have been a close friend of the local criminal leader Alexander Khabarov who died in prison in 2005.

27   Provided that the judgment is not challenged again.

court proceedings, the Archangel'sk Mayor Alexander Donskoy made numerous anti-Roma statements and promises to "solve the problem" regardless of
the final court ruling.

2.4. Antisemitism

While right-wing radicals may be debating the relevance of antisemitic
campaigning, they did not abandon such a tactic, but instead escalated antisemitism to a countrywide, high profile right-wing radical trend. Starting in
early 2005, scandalous antisemitic incidents followed one after another, restoring the nearly forgotten issue to the public discourse.

The kick-off event was the 13 January appeal signed by 19 State Duma
MPs of Rodina and Communist parties calling for the closure of all Jewish organizations in Russia, because, allegedly, these organizations all followed the
teachings of Kitsur Shulkhan Arukh. The authors of the appeal found hate
messages against non-Jews in an article published by Mikhail Nazarov back
in 2002. On the next day, the text of the appeal was published on Konstantin
Dushenov's Orthodox Russia newspaper website as a document open for
signature. The appeal already had 500 signatures as it was being put up on
the web.

A media scandal followed a week after the publication - on 22-23 January, just before the Russian president's visit to Poland to attend ceremonies
marking the 60th anniversary of the liberation of Auschwitz. Notably, President
Putin took some time to respond; his statement condemning the antisemitic
letter by the 19 MPs was made on 27 January in Poland and targeted the international, rather than the Russian, public.

Winter 2004-2005 was marked by an outburst of antisemitic violence in
Moscow. Hate-motivated violence against Jews had been rare before December 2004: only two incidents were reported over the previous 11 months
of 2004. In contrast, five attacks with an explicit antisemitic motive took place
during the 2004 – 2005 winter, injuring at least seven, including six in Moscow. The greatest public reverberation was caused by the attack on two rab-
bis – Alexander Lakshin and Ruven Kuravskiy – on 14 January. Almost all
such incidents in Moscow took place around the synagogue owned by the
Federation of Jewish Communities in Mar'ina Roscha. These incidents were

apparently the initiative of a local skinhead gang that chose to target Jews as opposed to Caucasus or Asian ethnicities (consequently, attacks against Jews in the neighborhood stopped immediately following the arrests of the suspected attackers of rabbi Lakshin). However, subsequent incidents - such as attack against an Israeli student, the antisemitic arson attack of a flat in St. Petersburg, and the harassment of Miss World 1998, an Israeli citizen, in the Moscow Metro - could have been provoked by the antisemitic petition and, most importantly, the subsequent lifting of taboo against public manifestations of antisemitism.

Other contributing factors included Russian journalists' unpreparedness for an educated discussion of relevant issues, and their lack of understanding of the real intentions of nationalist "patriots" who were able to use mass media as a propaganda instrument, rather than a forum for debate. A striking example of a journalist's professional failure in this respect was the 14 February 2005 TV talk show *K Bar'eru* [A Challenge to Duel] hosted by Vladimir Soloviev and involving Albert Makashov, known for his outrageous antisemitic pronouncements.

Subsequently, antisemitic propaganda continued at an alarming pace and assumed increasingly uncivilized forms, largely due to the inaction of law enforcement authorities, who refused to investigate the "Letter of Five Hundred" (later reviewed and resent to the prosecutor's office as the "Letter of Five Thousand") as a potential offence of incitement to ethnic hatred.

As their next step, antisemites attempted to rehabilitate the Blood Libel myth of ritual killings by Jews. The campaign was started, again, by Mikhail Nazarov, and linked to the disappearance and death of five school-age children in Krasnoyarsk. Nazarov publicly accused the Hassid community in Krasnoyarsk of ritual killings, and Governor Khloponin of covering up the crime. Soon this pronouncement was repeated – with the same impunity - at one of ethno-nationalist rallies held in Pushkin Square in Moscow.

The perfectly logical next step was the dissemination, since the autumn of 2005, of a documentary produced by Konstantin Dushenov and entitled "Russia with a Knife in Its Back: The Jewish Fascism and the Genocide of Russian People" (recently Dushenov has published more films with similar content on his website).

The year ended in a "monumental" scandal involving an attempt to erect a monument to Prince Svyatoslav in Belgorod region. A model of the would-be monument showed the Prince's horse stomping on a fallen Khazar warrior with the Star of David on his shield (which was obviously never used in the Khazar Kaganate; incidentally, a few people noticed a type of swastika on the Prince's shield). Ironically, the monument, rejected in 2005 by two regions, was to be erected in an Orthodox Christian monastery, even though Prince Svyatoslav was a pagan. The erection of the statue was stopped following protests by Jewish organizations across Russia. The author of the monument and the newly elected leader of the Union of Russian People Vyacheslav Klykov used the scandal to make another public statement to the effect that Jews were "enemies of Russia and Orthodoxy." He also refused to change the design of the monument, because *"we should understand the essence of Prince Svyatoslav's victory.*[28]*"*

This series of events appears to be more than the consistent escalation of antisemitic activity. It created the impression that antisemites were pushing certain informal boundaries of what is publicly acceptable, in order to check whether any reaction would follow. The failure of the prosecutorial office to find incitement to hatred encouraged antisemites to become more active, as perceived boundaries gradually faded in their minds. Incidentally, the behavior of Vladimir Zhirinovsky, the leader of the Liberal Democratic Party, is a good indicator of this loss of boundaries: his explicitly antisemitic pronouncements are increasingly heard at official events in Moscow,[29] whereas before they used to be more limited to his regional appearances.

Against this background, no one should be surprised by the scandal around antisemitic literature being distributed at the Moscow Book Fair in autumn, or by the fact that Valeriy Ganichev, known for his antisemitic views since Soviet times, was invited to sit in the Public Chamber, or by the antisemitic TV show *Our Strategy* being regularly broadcast on TV-3, or by other similar developments. These include open manifestations of aggression to-

---

28 However, commercial interests, apparently, prevailed: by unofficial reports, the six-pointed star was replaced by a twelve-pointed one, and in January 2006 the monument was opened in a low-profile ceremony.

29 For example, at the round table "Ethnic issues in the structure of social interaction" held in the State Duma on 16 May 2005.

wards Jews - as, for example, in Tambov, where on the eve of Passover, a group of teenagers with cropped hair yelled at a group of religious Jews, *"Yids!"* and *"Jude Schwein!"* or in Kursk, where a terrorist threat disrupted the performance of Mikhail Turetskiy's Jewish Choir. These also include increasingly targeted and emphatic vandalism. Thus, a kosher store was attacked in Moscow, while the Jewish cemetery in St. Petersburg has been systematically subjected to abuse by vandals. In total, in 2005, at least 27 acts of vandalism with regard to Jewish cultural and religious establishments were reported in 17 Russian regions.

Rather, we should be surprised that there have been relatively few incidents, and the attack against believers in a Moscow synagogue, injuring 8, happened on 11 January 2006 and not before, given the increasingly intense and cruel campaign against Jews over the last year.

2.5. Islamophobia

A wave of anti-Islamic acts continued throughout 2005, mainly in the form of vandalism against religious buildings and cemeteries. Mosques in Nizhniy Novgorod and in Penza were vandalized, and in Syktyvkar, on 1 December 2005, the building of the Komi Republic Muslim Religious Board was set on fire. However, we must admit that acts of vandalism against Muslim establishments in 2005 were less frequent than in 2004.

In 2005, attacks against individual Muslims,[30] apparently, were less frequent than in 2004, when an outburst of Islamophobia was provoked by the Beslan tragedy. It is important to note, however, the attack against a prayer house in Sergyev Posad. On 14 October, 2005, about a dozen skinheads armed with steel wire broke into a Muslim prayer house, yelling the slogans of "Russia for Russians!" and "Muslims have no place in Russia!" and attacked the believers. The head of the Muslim community was hospitalized following the attack.

Incidents of offensive public behavior against Muslims have been reported. On 3 September 2005 in Nizhniy Novgorod, Muslim organizers of a

---

30 This report does not cover persecutions of Muslims in the North Caucasus, e.g. in Kabardino-Balkariya. It would take a separate research project to study this subject.

meeting of silence to commemorate the Beslan tragedy were hissed by skin-heads yelling anti-Muslim slogans.

Aside from that, anti-Islamic sentiments were mostly manifested in public debates, becoming stronger in the second half of 2005. It all started with a discussion of an openly anti-Muslim novel by Yelena Chudinova, "The Mosque of Notre Dame." Later the debates became more intense following the November riots in Paris suburbs. The Russian media presented these events almost exclusively in terms of racial ("black immigrants and/or Arabs vs. white Europeans") and religious (specifically, religion/civilization) conflicts. In addition, statements by Muslim radicals saying that Russia must remove the cross from its coat of arms provoked even more aggressive anti-Muslim rhetoric.

Notably, unlike antisemitic publications that appeared in marginal media, anti-Islamic ones appeared in respectable print media with high circulation. Chudinova's book presentation was attended by Mikhail Leontyev, a well-known TV host, rather than by marginal nationalist "patriots." Moreover, following the Paris riots, a reference to "The Mosque of Notre Dame" was made by anti-liberal commentators, while Chudinova was for some time considered an established "expert on France."

While Russian society continues to find open support of antisemitism unacceptable, anti-Muslim pronouncements are increasingly well tolerated.

2.6. Other Religious Xenophobia

In addition to antisemitic and anti-Islamic incidents, religious xenophobia[31] was expressed mostly in numerous acts of vandalism with regard to cemeteries and religious buildings. Virtually all believers were affected, from smaller and newer faiths to the dominant Russian Orthodox Church. Notably, where vandalism is motivated by religious intolerance, rather than mere "hooliganism," attackers of the Orthodox Church (we documented about 30 anti-Orthodox acts of vandalism in 18 Russian regions), are mostly teenagers calling themselves "Satanists." In one case, in Vologda region, the slogan "Rus-

---

31   In this review, we do not cover discrimination of believers belonging to certain religious denominations.

sian gods for Russia!" were spray-painted on a burnt chapel, suggesting that left-wing radical neo-Pagans who often use this slogan were responsible for the initial arson.

The most serious incident took place in a small community near Vyazma (Smolensk region), where on 14 November an Orthodox chapel built next to a memorial to Soviet soldiers killed in WWII was blown up.

While the Russian Orthodox Church suffers from vandalism, members of other religious denominations are increasingly victimized by violence, often at the hands of people emphasizing their "Orthodoxy" or justifying violence by the need to protect "tradition" in the way they understand it.

For example, the increased activity of a few radical Orthodox groups seeking to terminate the Russian Orthodox Autonomous Church in Suzdal (Vladimir region) is considered to be the cause of attack against the elderly leader of the Autonomous Church, Metropolitan Valentin (Rusantsov) and systematic verbal offenses against the nuns of Rizopolozhensky Monastery of the Autonomous Church.

On 9 April, 2005, outside a Moscow club, a group armed with steel wire, chains and knives attacked black metal musicians and their fans; several people had to be hospitalized. The right-wing radical websites described the attackers as "Orthodox youth opposing the Satanists." On 10 August, in Pushkin Square in Moscow, a picket of Pentecostals was attacked by youths dressed in black shirts (according to some reports, members of the Eurasia Youth Union) shouting, "Burn the heretics!" and "Orthodoxy is our faith!" These attacks by essentially non-religious groups ostensibly guided by reli-gious motives were an alarming trend, especially noticeable last year.

2.7. Xenophobia as an Electoral Resource

As before, many politicians continued to regard xenophobic sentiments shared by many Russians as an effective electoral resource. Virtually all elec-tion campaigns in 2005 featured candidates who exploited ethno-nationalist slogans in some way. One can distinguish a few main types of xenophobia-based campaigning.

An old and well-known type of negative PR is based on the use of xenophobic slogans and materials to discredit the opponent. Such negative

PR can be anonymous, as, for example, in Buryatia, where campaign posters of a candidate standing for the Mayor's office in the city of Gusinoozersk were covered with stickers saying "Down with the Buryat!".[32] Or it can be more sophisticated, when xenophobic materials are disseminated on behalf of the opponent - during municipal elections in Tula, for example, xenophobic leaflets were disseminated on behalf of the local Armenian National-cultural autonomy.[33]

Participation in elections is a legal opportunity for small and little-known right-wing radical groups to expand their audience, even if they do not expect to win the elections anyway. The election campaign season gives them the means to promote their ideas on a large scale - including free airtime on television. This was the reason behind the election campaigns of the Leningrad region NDPR activists as well as the openly neo-Nazi National Socialist Society and the Freedom Party.

Sometimes more than one right-wing radical candidate would stand for elections in the same district and some would withdraw in favor of the strongest. This happened, for example, during the additional elections to the State Duma from Preobrazhensky Electoral District No 199 in Moscow, where the candidates included Colonel Kvachkov accused of attempted assassination of Chubais, and Alexey Nazarov, a neo-Nazi politician supported by the National Socialist Society whose campaigning during at least two meetings left no doubts as to his neo-Nazi orientation. Just two days before the vote, A. Nazarov withdrew from the elections in favor of Kvachkov. In this particular case, we are not interested in the reasons for his withdrawal,[34] but instead in the demonstration of an efficient method of expanding the scope of xenophobia-based campaigning. The campaign was doubled in volume, while only one candidate remained on the election day, avoiding an even minimal scat-

---

32   The elections were held on 18 October 2005.
33   "Tul'skie armyane trebuyut nakazat' provokatorov" (Armenians in Tula demand that provocateurs be punished). *Agenstvo National'nykh Novostey*, 25 October 2005. (http://www.annews.ru/modules.php?name=News&file=article&sid=19554).   The elections were held on 30 October 2005.
34   However, if the suspicion is true that the decision had been made under pressure from Kvachkov's HQ (i.e. DPNI and NDPR), we can assume that skinheads (the National Socialist Society is closer to skinhead groups than to parties) are bound by some sort of "party discipline."

tering of the votes.

More reputable candidates with good chances for success also resort to explicitly xenophobic rhetoric. As a rule, they regard xenophobic messages as a campaigning tool, rather than the basis of their campaigning. The scandal that xenophobic campaigning will inevitably cause is an effective promotional strategy, helping to break through the powerful information blockade faced by all movements and candidates other than those belonging to United Russia.

The Rodina Party used this strategy to the greatest effect during the Moscow City Duma election campaign. The scandal exceeded the wildest expectations of those political advisors who had chosen this strategy for Rodina. The slogans "Moscow for Muscovites!" and "Let us clean the city of garbage!" immediately attracted media attention. A picket held by Rodina Party in October in Mayakovsky Square in Moscow featured young people "sweeping out" immigrant workers from Moscow streets. The youth chapter of the party adopted a new name –"Patriotic Greenpeace" – seeking to "clean" open-air markets in Moscow of dishonest immigrant salesmen. The scandal peaked when the party televised its campaign video titled "Let us clean the city of garbage", where "garbage" was understood as migrants of non-Russian ethnicity.

Rodina's campaigning strategy offended many people exposed to it, not to mention that it almost provoked a diplomatic scandal (the embassies of Azerbaijan and France expressed their indignation).[35] So D. Rogozin reached his goal – the information blockade was broken, the scandal was the most noticeable part of the Moscow Duma election campaign, while Rodina is now seen –rightly or wrongly – as a powerful competitor of United Russia.

The rulings of the Moscow City Court and then of the Russian Supreme Court to ban Rodina Party from elections for "incitation of ethnic hatred" were apparently totally unexpected. This is the *first* known case in Russia of banning a party from elections for this reason. Before, parties had been sometimes banned on formal grounds (as for example, the Spas Bloc in the 1999

---

35   The French ambassador was indignant that Rodina modified its video following the ban by translating the content into French and thus alluding to the riots in France.

parliamentary elections).

Nevertheless, Rodina was not the only party that used xenophobic slogans in this campaign. The party actually borrowed the idea from the LDPR
that had, on many occasions, camouflaged ethnic xenophobia by using geographic and social terminology in its slogans like "Criminal Southerners – get
out of Russia!", "It is not Caucasus here," and others.[36] The recent election
campaign was not an exception – the best-known piece of promotion was a
leaflet published by the Liberal Democratic Party, that proclaimed "Shut off
Moscow from Southerners! We are [standing up] for a city with Russian faces.
Illegal [immigrants] have no place in the capital."

As a result, in November 2005, Rodina and the LDPR sued each other
for their virtually identical type of campaigning, demanding that the opponent
be banned from the elections. The Liberal Democrats won, and Rodina lost.
Unfortunately, this outcome supports the widespread opinion that the real
reason for banning Rodina from the Moscow elections was not its nationalism, but its popularity in the city and, consequently, its potentially successful
competition with United Russia.

Another example was the campaign for the head of the administration
office in Megion – a city in Khanty-Mansiiskiy Autonomous District. Alexander
Kuzmin, a strong candidate for the office, left the current Mayor, Alexander
Chepaykin of United Russia, far behind after the first round (49.53% vs.
27.33%, respectively). A. Kuz'min relied heavily on xenophobic sentiments in
his campaign. On 8 April 2005, literally on the eve of the second round of vot-
ing, the District Court ruled, following long and confusing proceedings, that A.
Kuzmin must be banned from elections for *"bribery, incitation of ethnic hatred
and racial discrimination."* The elections were cancelled, the city has not had a
Mayor since, and Kuz'min took his case to the Supreme Court (the Court overruled the previous decision to ban the candidate, finding procedural irregulari-
ties). However, the Supreme Court refused to clear the candidate of ethnic hatred charges.

Rogozin responded to Azeri ambassador's note by rather rude polemics, but
stopped short of further offending the French ambassador.

36   To remind the reader, this strategy was used by the LDPR at least three times in
2004. It was challenged in court twice, but the party's campaigning was found legal
both times.

To reiterate, the Rodina Party and A. Kuz'min cases are unique for Russia's electoral practices. To put them into perspective, we should remember that in 2003, candidate German Sterligov openly called to shoot Roma and Azeri in Moscow streets, but the court failed to find "incitation of ethnic hatred." The political motives underlying both judgments virtually set off their anti-xenophobic component and demonstrated that the law was applied selectively to suppress rivals of "the ruling political party."

In all other cases, electoral xenophobia remains unpunished, even if physical fighting is involved, as was the case in Vladimir region. During the Communist Party leader Zyuganov's meeting with voters, Igor Artyomov from the Russian All-Nation Union launched a verbal attack against Magomed Akhmadov, leader of local Young Communists, by targeting Akhmadov's Chechen ethnicity. Magomed Akhmadov, in turn, called Artyomov "fascist" and the latter hit him in the face. Currently, a criminal investigation against Artyomov is ongoing, but it is highly unlikely that the popular nationalist politician will be punished.

Notably, electoral outcomes for right-wing radicals are usually negligible, except for rare cases, where other, mostly subjective factors come into play.[37] However, by the end of 2005 this situation started to change in an alarming way. One example is the aforementioned additional elections in District 199 in Moscow, where Colonel Kvachkov's campaign was based on the slogans of a "national liberation war" against the *"foreign occupant government"* of present-day Russia. Specifically, he said: *"Destroying the occupants and their collaborators is not a crime, but the duty and responsibility of every defender of our Fatherland loyal to his military oath."* Certainly, all voters in the district knew that the Colonel faced political terrorism charges for the assassination attempt against Chubais, so at least the 44,167 people who voted for Kvachkov approved of his terrorist act. A major part of "Kvachkov's constituency" also knew his political views, because Kvachkov's "manifesto of national-patriotic rebellion" was widely covered in the press. Consequently,

---

37   A detailed analysis of reasons for electoral success of right-wing candidates is given by V. Pribylovskiy in his report "Natsional-patrioty na regional'nykh vyborakh, 2004–2004 gg." (National Patriots in regional elections, 2000–2004) at the conference *"Russkaya natsionalisticheskaya tematika i vybory, 1993 – 2004".* (Russian nationalism and elections, 1993–2004). Moscow, 17-18 February, 2005.

some members of the constituency voted for Kvachkov as a right-wing radical. So, V. Kvachkov with 28.9% vote was a national-patriotic candidate successfully competing with the "ruling party candidate." The former "Spetsnaz"
[Special Purpose Forces] serviceman Kvachkov lost to Sergey Shavrin, a
former "Spetsnaz" man too, by a mere 7%. Coupled with the striking success
of Vladimir Popov, a formerly little-known neo-Nazi candidate – 4.18% vote –
in the Moscow City Duma elections, we can see that the December 2005
elections in Moscow demonstrated an unprecedentedly large growth of radical xenophobia in the Russian capital - and possibly, in the entire country.

2.8. Radical Nationalism on Behalf of the State

As in the past, rather radical manifestations of ethno-nationalism by
agents of the state were reported again in 2005.

In most cases, those responsible were the legislators who are more diverse in their background and behavior than bureaucrats. Members of the
Liberal Democratic Party retain their image of nationalists. One illustrative example was the draft law proposed by Nikolai Kuryanovich of the LDPR to de-
prive Russian women who marry foreigners of Russian citizenship. The racist
nature of the draft – enthusiastically supported by the party leader Zhirinovsky
– left no doubts: the underlying concern was for "protecting the gene pool"
from being "corrupted" – even if the woman later decides to get a divorce and
come back to Russia.

MPs do not stop short of contacts with neo-Nazis. For example, the
Slavic Union leader Dmitry Demushkin regularly meets with MPs who willingly
keep photos with a neo-Nazi handshake (S. Baburin) or even openly state
that skinheads are "useful" and raise their arms in the Nazi greeting (the said
Kuryanovich).

The tough control of United Russia over the entire parliament does not
prevent the communist MP and ex-governor of Krasnodar Nikolai
Kondratenko from systematic verbal attacks against "Zionists" at every plenary.[38] The mentioned congress of the Union of Russian People in Novem-

---

38   The United Russia's specific methods of conducting the Duma plenary sessions,
      and MPs xenophobic rhetoric were discussed on 25 October 2005 at a conference

ber, alongside the expected N. Kuryanovich and S. Baburin, also featured speakers like Sergey Glazyev who distanced himself from even a moderate version of nationalism displayed by his colleague Dmitry Rogozin.

However, this phenomenon was not limited to parties such as Rodina, the LDPR or CPRF (with its spin-off, Gennady Semigin's Patriots of Russia) known for their members' xenophobic attitudes, or to participation of right-wing radicals in formal events organized by government - for example, in Archangelsk, Leningrad and Pskov regions.

A new and alarming trend in 2005 was the consistent effort of the state to "domesticate" skinheads through various pro-presidential youth groups, primarily through the Nashi movement. A few years ago, the press reported close links between Nashi's predecessors Iduschie Vmeste ("Those who march together") and skinheads; we have no reasons to assume that they had lost contact. Their leader, Vassily Yakemenko, said on many occasions that Nashi were prepared to "work" with skinheads for their "reformation." How are the "nashists" - whose congress at the Lake Seliger featured talks by the former leader of the extremist Ukrainian group UNA-UNSO Dmitro Korchinsky - are going to "reform" skinheads is anyone's guess. Moreover, the movement has had close links with the Gladiator security agency, which in turn is connected with Spartak soccer fans known for their extreme aggressiveness and right-wing attitudes. As a result of this collaboration, at least one person was beaten, Ilya Yashin, activist of the liberal Oborona group who secretly attended the founding congress of Nashi. "Nashists" and "gladiators" are the suspected attackers of leftist youth (mainly National Bolsheviks, NBP) outside Avtozavodskaya Metro Station in Moscow in August 2005.

The Moscow City Government launched a strange, to say the least, initiative in August 2005, when the City Department of Justice registered a new NGO, the Moscow Association of Sports Fans. The objectives of the new organization include, among others, *"combating terrorism, extremism and chauvinism."* It was expected that the new organization would bring together

---

of the Franco-Russian Center for Social Studies "Russky natsionalizm v ofitsial'nykh strukturakh rossiyskogo gosudarstva" (Russian nationalism in official structures of the Russia,) in particular in Yekaterina Mikhailovskaya's presentation entitled "Natsionalisticheskiy diskurs v Dume na primere partii 'Rodina'" (Nationalist discourse in the Duma: the Rodina Party example).

fans of seven soccer clubs - CSCA, Spartak, Dynamo, Torpedo, Locomotive, FC Moscow, and Saturn of Moscow region. The most active fans of these clubs, especially Spartak and CSCA fans, are not only extremely aggressive, but maintain close links with a number of skinhead groups, so much so that the law enforcement agencies hardly see any difference between soccer fans and skinheads. It is unlikely that soccer fans bundled by bureaucrats in an association will suddenly become less aggressive to anyone they perceive as alien.

The examples above show clearly that the government's "fight for youth" is characterized either by lack of education about youth subcultures, or by extreme unscrupulousness. Ultimately, both will lead to the same outcome, i.e. a demonstration of impunity of anyone who is "patriotic" and loyal to the current regime. There are more facts, besides the stories of nashists and soccer fans, to prove it. In Voronezh, law enforcement authorities were surprised that a youth gang with a name suggestive of neo-Nazi themes – the White Patrol – which *"supported the system"* was, in fact, involved in the killing of a student from Peru. The law enforcement said, *"... we did not expect it from Vityaz and the White Patrol; the youngsters have come together for a good cause – they practice sports and fight drugs."* At the end of summer in Moscow, a hard rock music festival was held under the auspices of the United Russia Party. Originally, its slogan was "Long Live Russia!", but then the organizers, apparently, realized that it was a traditional slogan of radical nationalists and replaced it with a more neutral "Long live Russia, Long live Moscow!" The concert program featured Sergey "Spider" Troitsky, an icon of Russian skinheads. The slogan of the festival combined with the performance of Troitsky's group Corrosion of Metal appears to be intended to please skinheads.

Some prominent politicians in Russia allowed using their names in right-wing radical promotion. For example, Konstantin Dushenov advertised his antisemitic film using a collection of quotations from various political, civil and religious leaders, mostly known for their antisemitism, but others as well. For example, he quoted from speeches made by Lyubov Sliska, Vice Speaker of the State Duma (United Russia). It was easy for the Vice Speaker to find it out and respond, but there was no public response on her part.

Another example of "silent endorsement" was the speech of the Federation Council Speaker Sergey Mironov on the "Two to One" TV show, where the show hosts were pushing the politician to discuss what they termed an anti-Russian "*conspiracy of Jewish oligarchs*" (a quote from their conversation). While Mironov only said a few words about Boris Berezovsky's political role, he failed to make any comments or challenge the TV hosts about the nationalist context that they imposed on the discussion. Sergey Mironov, technically the third most important political figure in the country, virtually legitimized antisemitic pronouncements by taking part in the talk show.

3.   Opposition to Radical Nationalism

3.1. NGO Activities and Spontaneous Opposition

Opposition to the increasingly prominent radical nationalism in the country has always been an important part of NGO activism, but their capacity is limited. Most NGOs operate within traditional spheres of research, awareness-raising, education, and expert services targeted at diverse audiences, including graduate students, journalists, school students, police, teachers and officials.

In 2005, however, NGOs focused increasingly on "street actions" to raise public awareness. Actions that featured young people painting over xenophobic graffiti in Russian cities were especially popular and widespread. Other actions included anti-fascist pickets and rallies, the largest of them being the "Anti-fascist March" on 18 December 2005 attended by about 1500 people, including, in addition to members of human rights groups and other NGOs, representatives of various political parties and movements, mostly of the liberal orientation.

Spontaneous opposition to radical nationalists is increasingly common - in particular, a number of cases were reported throughout the year of nationalist campaigners being ousted from social protest rallies (i.e. in Noginsk outside Moscow, and in Pskov), and of unorganized people spontaneously destroying nationalist leaflets and graffiti. A number of times, those whom skinheads attempted to target, responded by fighting back. For example, in

Kursk, on the first day of 2005, local residents taking a stroll downtown, offended by the neo-Nazi slogans, attacked and beat the skinheads who were
shouting at them. In May, a few skinheads were beaten by passengers of a
Moscow suburban train, whom the youngsters tried to involve in some "action" (apparently, in a violent racist attack). In contrast, in Kaluga region, passengers in a suburban train did not beat the skinheads, but escorted them to
a police station; by doing so, the citizens prevented a riot that the skinheads
had planned on that day.

Opposition between skinheads and leftist youth has been growing both
in scale and in intensity, including the growth of violence frequently provoked
by the young left-wing anti-fascists. Their attacks, while motivated by a sin-
cere desire to fight neo-Nazis, are as illegal as the violence of their opponents, and lead nowhere, except even more violence and more victims. Thus,
for example, on 16 December, a group of leftist youth attacked a club where a
music festival featuring Corrosion of Metal was taking place. Massive fighting
followed, leaving many victims, mostly the anti-fascists themselves and members of the audience who had nothing to do with the skinheads.

3.2. Criminal Prosecution of Right-Wing Radicals

Undoubtedly, law enforcement authorities must play the central role in
combating illegal manifestations of the right-wing radicalism. Notably, they
were much more active in 2005 than before, at least in the criminal prosecution of offenders, particularly for violent crimes. While in 2003 only four convictions took account of the hate motive, in 2004 there were nine such convictions, and in 2005 their number reached 17 (in Moscow (two), Moscow region, and St. Petersburg - two convictions in each city - Blagoveschensk,
Vladivostok, Volgograd, Yekaterinburg, Lipetsk, Murmansk, Perm', Saratov,
Surgut and Tambov). A total of 60 persons were found guilty in the above trials, but only 50 convictions addressed the hate motive.

Most offenders were sentenced to actual, rather than probation, prison
terms; only four defendants of the Schultz-88 and Mad Crowd trials in St. Petersburg and one defendant each in Lipetsk and Murmansk got probation
sentences. This is important, because, as we know from experience, probation sentences do not discourage skinheads from subsequent offences, but

give offenders a renewed sense of impunity; many of those convicted in 2005 had already received past probation sentences for violent attacks and vandalism. An example is the story of Yuri Zavershinsky, a skinhead from Lipetsk. In August 2004, he was sentenced to two years of probation under article 213 (misdemeanor, or "hooliganism") for an armed attack against a Mozambican. Then, although investigators found Nazi literature in his home, they did not find the attack against the African to be racist, and the criminal investigator told the local press that he was not going to bring charges under art. 282, because it would be *political.*" However, seven months after the sentence, on 14 March 2005, Yuri Zavershinsky together with three companions – one of them previously convicted for banditry – beat a man from Mali. This time, the attackers were sentenced under article 282 part 2.a of the Criminal code to 2 and 4.5 years of prison.

Another sign of progress in the prosecution of violent racist crimes was the fact that courts actively applied not only this paragraph of article 282 of the Criminal Code, but other Criminal Code articles which punish for violent crimes and cite the motive of racial hatred among aggravating circumstances. At least eight[39] out of 16 sentences in cases heard by jury courts under article 105 (murder) and 111 (inflicting serious injuries) took into account this aggravating circumstance.[40] We note in particular the sentencing of a skinhead group in Saratov. In February 2005, a jury in Saratov found three local skinheads guilty of a murder motivated by ethnic hatred (the cases of two more persons involved in the killing were investigated separately under different proceedings). However, a few months later the Russian Supreme Court overruled the sentence due to procedural violations, and sent it back to be reconsidered by other judges. By that time, the other investigation had been completed, the cases were combined, and in September 2005 a new panel of judges sentenced all the five defendants to prison terms ranging between 5 and 13 years.

The motive of racial hatred was also involved in a number of criminal prosecutions opened in 2005 into the vandalism of cemeteries. Two of the

---

39   We do not know the exact wording of charges and sentences in some cases.

trials have by now resulted in convictions. In December, two "Satanists" from Naberezhnye Chelny were found guilty of vandalism, and in Astrakhan region in May, three ethnic Chechens were found guilty of vandalizing a rural cemetery in Yandyki. The latter were sentenced to 18 months in a correctional colony, but the sentence was then replaced by a probation term. This ruling provoked the anti-Chechen riot in August 2005 described above.

Notably, about a half of sentences in 2005 were for offences committed in 2002 and 2003. Long proceedings into serious crimes are common for Russian courts, but a court in Volgograd set a record of slowness: a group of 13 skinheads were on trial for murders and beatings of persons from Central Asia, offences which had been committed back in 2002.[41] The case file was sent to court on 30 May 2003, the trial started in January 2004, and the sentences were passed in April 2005. During the time elapsed since the investigation was opened, the Criminal Code was amended, and three of the defendants were released without trial. Nevertheless, eight of the nine remaining defendants were sentenced to prison terms ranging between 4 and 10 years.[42] Notably, this high profile trial and the strict sentences taking into account the racist motives, served as a deterrent for skinheads in Volgograd. These radicals refrained from "actions" for a number of months, because punishment was now a real, rather than an abstract prospect.

The trial of Schultz-88 group in St. Petersburg was also very long, taking a few years. Schultz-88 activists were detained back in 2003 and charges were brought against them promptly, including, for the first time in Russia, charges under the new article 282[1] (organization of, or involvement in, an extremist community, added in 2002). This highly publicized trial was apparently designed to demonstrate how strict law enforcement authorities are with regard to racists. However, it ended in surprisingly soft sentences – one of the defendants was acquitted, and three others received probation terms. In addi-

---

40   In another trial involving cruel murders of Uzbek migrant workers in the summer of 2004, the Moscow Region Prosecutor's Office was not able to prove the hate motive. It is important, however, that they were prepared to bring these charges.

41   However, the record is likely to be beaten by the Rodoshkevich group trial in Novosibirsk. The group was charged with a series of attacks against migrants from Central Asia back in 2002. Members of the group were arrested in November 2002. The proceedings started in October 2003 and are still ongoing.

42   One was found not guilty.

tion, the proceedings took so long that charges of involvement in an extremist community had to be lifted, because the statute of limitations had expired by the time of trial. Only the group's leader, Dmitry Bobrov, was sentenced to an actual prison term for a number of charges, including the organization of an extremist community.

In some cases, sentencing for racist attacks still failed to take the hate motive into account. We know of at least six such sentences (in Moscow, Krasnodar,[43] Togliatti, Novosibirsk, Sverdlovsk and Voronezh). The trial in Sverdlovsk region presented a particularly strange example.

In December 2005, a local court convicted a group of teenagers who killed three Armenian migrant workers in May 2005. After the killings, the youngsters came back to a local cafe and publicly declared that they had just performed a "cleansing operation" in the city.[44] Regardless of this fact, the court did not even consider the ethnic hatred as a motive of the crime. In this case, mentioning the qualifying circumstance of ethnic hatred in the indictment would not mean a harsher punishment (the sentence was the harshest possible anyway – from 10 years to life in prison), but would be appropriate from the legal perspective and likely to produce an educational and awareness-raising effect. The punishment, in this case, would be administered to racist killers, rather than "delinquent youth."

Of course, many racist offences are never detected.

While the law enforcement authorities increasingly prosecute violent racist crimes, things are not as straightforward with regard to ethno-nationalist "propaganda."

Certainly, prosecution of those responsible for such propaganda increased in 2005 with 12 trials[45] against 15 defendants[46] ending in convictions

---

43 However, given the specific situation in Krasnodar Territory, the mere fact that the matter of the killings of Meskhetian Turks reached the court and ended in convictions is a positive thing in and of itself.

44 Notably, they were detained only after the incident caused an international scandal: the Armenian ambassador was in Sverdlovsk region with an official visit at the time of the killings.

45 These statistics include sentences where the defendants were found guilty, but were not punished under art. 282 due to expiry of the statute of limitations. There were three such cases in 2005: Victor Korchagin in Moscow, Ram Latypov in Khabarovsk and Alexander Nikolaenko (his first case) in Kemerovo.

(as opposed to just three in 2004). In 2005, Kemerovo region was the absolute leader in terms of such convictions with four sentences and only one of them was probation. Promoters of racial hatred were also convicted in Kirov, Moscow, Novgorod, Nalchik, Oryol, Syktyvkar, Ekaterinburg and Khabarovsk.

As a form of punishment, courts also started to ban the type of activity defendants are charged with. In 2005, two such sentences were passed; the first, involving the National Bolshevik Alexander Nikolayenko,[47] was passed on 26 April 2005 in Kemerovo region. The second, passed on 31 May 2005 in Novgorod deserves a special mention, being the first conviction under article 282^1 (organization of an extremist community) in Russian jurisprudence, and we consider the sentence passed by the Novgorod court to be the best ruling in a racial hatred case in the recent years.

Back in 2004, three RNE activists were charged with composing and disseminating a newsletter entitled *Novgorodets* containing hate texts. The investigators, and subsequently the judges, found the defendants to constitute an extremist community, and their actions were qualified under articles 282 part 2 and 282^1. Their leader, Mikhail Pekin, was convicted under part 1 (as the main organizers), and the other two under part 2 (as participants). The sentence (four, three and two years of prison, respectively) was probation, but all three were banned by the court from distributing any mass media materials for three years, and Pekin was banned from working as a journalist for the same period.

Three more people, in addition to these four, were substantially punished. We regard it as tangible progress, because none of the three persons convicted in 2004 were ultimately punished.

Of the six "real" sentences (three in Kemerovo region, one each in Novgorod, Sverdlovsk region and Kirov), only two involved prison terms. The first was passed in October in Sverdlovsk region, although the defendant sen-

---

46   One man out of the 13 - A. Nikolaenko - was convicted twice.

47   There were two trials involving Nikolaenko and running simultaneously; in both cases, he was charged under articles 280 and 282 of the Criminal Code, but for different publications. The first sentence was passed in April 2005 - then Nikolaev was found guilty under article 282, but the statute of limitations had expired, so he was sentenced only under article 280 to a probation term combined with a ban on engaging in journalism. The second sentence – six months of prison – was under both articles of the Criminal Code.

tenced to six months in a prison colony was arrested at the time already facing even more serious charges of hate-motivated violence.[48] The other conviction was the second sentence over the three-month period handed out to
the National Bolshevik A. Nikolaenko - again, six months in a settlement colony.

The remaining four sentences did not involve incarceration. In addition
to being banned from certain occupations, the defendants were sentenced
either to correctional labor (for someone already employed it means that part
of their salary is withheld) or to fines. We believe that courts were correct in
their sentencing.

Six more people were found guilty, but either their sentences were probation, or the statutory limitation period had expired (we should note that the
defendants were not the responsible for the delays, although they were certainly interested in exhausting the period of limitation, but the prosecutors and
judges were – they who did not know how to deal with it[49]). The lack of real,
rather than virtual, punishments encouraged new waves of xenophobic
statements. Thus in 2005, Pavel Ivanov from Novgorod and Igor Kolodezenko
from Novosibirsk resumed the activities they had received probation sentences for (the latter - even two sentences over the recent years) under article
282 of the Criminal Code. Vladimir Popov from Vologda continued publishing
his antisemitic paper "Slavyansky Nabat," and prosecution against him was
apparently dropped. Victor Korchagin,[50] who on several occasions was found
guilty under the "incitation of ethnic hatred" provision but never actually punished, continued speaking at rallies and accusing Jews of ritual killings even
though his trial was ongoing. Sergey Lukyanenko, an antisemitic publisher in

---

48   It follows from media reports that the incident in question involved a series of arson
     attacks against cafes owned by "people from the Caucasus" in the autumn of 2004
     in Yekaterinburg and Verkhnyaya Pyshma, killing one and seriously injuring at least
     one person who required hospitalization. We do not know, however, which of the
     arsons the defendant was involved in.
49   See a detailed analysis of reasons why such cases are difficult in: Ratinov A., Kroz
     A., Ratinova N. *Otvetstvennost' za razzhiganie vrazhdy i nenavisti* (Liability for Incit-
     ing Animosity and Hatred). Moscow: Yurlitinform, 2005. pp. 12–16.
50   In early 2005, an appeal court confirmed his release from punishment due to expiry
     of the statute of limitations. However, the expiry is very doubtful, because all the
     time Korchagin continued distributing the materials like the ones he was prosecuted
     for.

Khabarovsk, continued his activity in spite of being currently on probation and being accused for the third consecutive time under article 282.

Undoubtedly, prosecutions under article 282 can be challenging, given that the investigators usually lack special training or experience with regard to this rather specific type of offences. They often request expert opinions from the wrong experts, who, in turn, make mistakes in their assessments.[51] Therefore, the prosecutor's case in court is usually weak in this type of trial. A solution may involve re-organizing the way prosecutors operate.

At times, it is nearly impossible to get authorities to prosecute, not to speak of conviction and sentencing. The following requests for prosecution were denied:

-    against the author and promoters of the antisemitic "Letter of 500" (by now reaching "15,000") containing an explicitly discriminatory demand that all Jewish organizations must be closed in Russia; the demand was based on a series of old antisemitic myths (request to prosecute denied twice);

-    against organizers and speakers at the antisemitic meeting in Pushkin Square in Moscow, where Hassids were accused of ritual killings of children;

-    against Mikhail Nazarov for an antisemitic book and a series of publications (one of the reasons given for the refusal to prosecute was that the book *"was not only officially allowed by the [Russian Orthodox] Church to be sold in its bookstores, but was recognized as a 1999 bestseller. Books which incite hatred are not blessed for publication by the highest Orthodox hierarchy."*)

None of these publications was found by prosecutors to provoke ethnic hatred.

Another less known, but illustrative case was the refusal to open a criminal investigation into the publication in the Pskov region of the newspaper "The Catechism of a Jew in the USSR" – an antisemitic fabrication known since Soviet times; back in 1995 the aforementioned Victor Korchagin was

---

51   Ratinov A., Kroz A., Ratinova N. *Otvetstvennost' za razzhiganie vrazhdy i nenavisti* (Liability for Inciting Animosity and Hatred). Moscow: Yurlitinform, 2005. pp. 187–236.

convicted for its publication.

The Catechism example demonstrates that the same texts are assessed differently depending on the time and on the specific prosecutor. However, in 2005 there was an example of the same text being assessed differently by the same prosecutorial office within the same month. On 4 March 2005, the City Prosecutor's Office in St. Petersburg warned the newspapers "Orthodox Russia" and "For the Russian Cause" about the publication of "The letter of 500" inciting ethnic hatred, but in April the same prosecutors refused to open a criminal investigation under article 282 of the Criminal Code into the same incident. The reason given for their refusal to prosecute was not that a warning had been issued or that the offence was not dangerous enough for criminal prosecution,[52] but inter alia, that as long as there were no "calls to commit illegal acts against members of a certain ethnicity, race or religion," there was no crime under article 282 – an interpretation, which is not based on the Criminal Code.

3.3. Administrative Liability and Preventive Actions

Administrative sanctions are increasingly used against right-wing radicals – in addition to law enforcement authorities, other authorized government bodies may impose administrative liability.

Increasingly, we hear about administrative punishment for the display of Nazi or similar symbols and paraphernalia (art. 20.3 of the Russian Code of Administrative Offences). Such cases were reported in Oryol, Murmansk, Moscow (a participant of the Right March was sentenced to five days of administrative arrest), Ryazan region and Krasnodar territory.

After a long delay caused by the ongoing administrative reform, prosecutors and RosOkhranKul'tura resumed their warnings to mass media for ethno-religious xenophobia. We know of at least 11 such warnings issued in 2005 (six by RosOkhranKul'tura and five by prosecutors),[53] while in 2004

---

52   In principle, it is possible that an offensive publication may cause the media company to be closed, without a criminal prosecution against the author or the publisher.

53   It remains unclear if "*Rus' pravoslavnaya*" (Orthodox Russia) and "*Za russkoe delo*" (For the Russian Cause) were warned by RosOkhranKul'tura. If both publications

there were only four warnings.[54] As a rule, editorial offices do not stop their ethno-nationalist publications after such warnings, but at least they become nervous. As of this writing (January 2006), at least five warnings issued in 2005 are being challenged in courts.

Table 2:   Warnings by the Russian government and judiciary of xenophobic media outlets

ROSOKHRANKUL'TURA		PROSECUTORS	
WARNED MEDIA	*NOTE*	*WARNED MEDIA*	*NOTE*
Zakuban'e (Transku-ban Region) (Ady-geya)		*Era Rossii (Russia's Era)* (Moscow)	
Volzhskaya Zarya (Volga Dawn) (Sa-mara region)	Successfully challenged in court in Janu-ary 2006	*Ya russkiy v Samare (I am [ethnic] Russian in Samara)* (Samara region)	Challenged in court
Ya russkiy v Samare (I am [ethnic] Rus-sian in Samara) (Samara region)	Challenged in court	*Za russkoe delo (For the Russian Cause)* (St. Petersburg)	Challenged in court
Russkaya Pravda (Russian Truth) (Moscow)		*Rus' pravoslavnaya (The Orthodox Rus)* (St. Petersburg)	
Kurs (The Course) (Kemerovo region)	Warned for inciting to so-cial strife	*Moskovskie Vorota (Moscow Gates)* (Kaluga region)	Challenged in court
Nevskiy TV Channel (St. Petersburg)			

---

received two warnings each (from RosOkhranKul'tura and prosecutors), then a total of 13 warnings were issued in 2005.

54   Only warnings concerning inciting ethnic and religious hatred are meant here.

Notably, such warnings had been rarely challenged in courts before; only well-respected mainstream media did so, rather than marginal nationalist publications. Now all of them seem to realize that an unchallenged warning may lead to the media company being closed. Indeed, on 4 July 2005, Khamovnichesky Court in Moscow closed NBP's *General'naya Liniya* paper following three warnings in 2004.[55] However, a list of media warned in 2005 shows that xenophobic statements in respectable mainstream publications went unnoticed by prosecutors and RosOkhranKul'tura. This seems strange, because *Komsomolskaya Pravda* and *Moskovsky Komsomolets*, not to mention a number of regional periodicals, published numerous offensive articles ranging from xenophobic to explicitly racist in 2005.[56]

Right-wing radical organizations did not feel much pressure either – we do not know of a single liquidation of such organizations through judicial proceedings in 2005 – or in 2004, for that matter. In contrast to the previous years, we have not heard of any right-wing radical groups having been liquidated on formal grounds (such as a failure to submit requested reports to the registering authority, etc.).

There was one example of an organization officially warned by the prosecutor for extremist activity[57] in April 2005 – the Krasnodar chapter of the neo-Heathen organization "Spiritual Ancestral Russian Empire". The group has declared itself sovereign and separate from the Russian Federation. It arbitrarily "grants" lands and property to its members, and encourages them to defend their property using weapons. While the group's rhetoric and activities are rather weird and raise doubts about mental sanity of its members, it is not as harmless as may appear. It is responsible for at least one riot in September 2004 in Krasnodar Territory. In April 2005, the same organization condemned to death the Russian Vice Premier Alexander Zhukov (for facilitating a *"Judo-Nazi occupation"*) and called upon its members to execute the sentence *"using*

---

55   Two of them were for "extremism" and one for inciting ethnic hatred (and perfectly justified).
56   See, the section *"Yazyk vrazhdy v rossiyskikh SMI"* (Hate Speech in Russian Media) on the SOVA Center website at http://xeno.sova-center.ru/213716E.
57   It is also known that a few warnings were issued in Tatarstan, but there is no information as to whom and when they were issued.

all available means, in any form, and at any convenient time.[58]

We know of one denial of registration to a non-governmental association: on 15 September 2005, the Federal Registration Service in St. Petersburg and Leningrad region refused to register NDPR's new organization, the National Imperial Path of Russia, because its charter contained hate-provoking statements. This decision of the registering authority in St. Petersburg is notable, particularly considering that a month later another branch of the same organization using the same charter was registered in Moscow without problems (see above).

Legal remedies continue to be rarely used against right-wing radical organizations and publications. For the last couple of years, no NGOs have been liquidated specifically for nationalist activities, and very few media outlets were closed for the same reason.[59] The case of *General'naya Liniya* having been closed for nationalism is questionable: firstly, the second level court has not yet confirmed the ruling, so it is not in effect yet; and secondly, nationalism was not the first on the list of charges against NBP's paper. The main legal and political reason for suppressing NBP is its extreme opposition to the current government.

In addition to criminal and administrative sanctions against right-wing radicals, increased focus was placed on preventing manifestations of right-wing radicalism. In July, a local court in charge of Yu. Zavershinsky's case (see above) issued a special order to the city administration of Lipetsk prescribing increased control over *Vityaz'* Sports Club as a potential meeting place of local neo-Nazis. An example of preventive policing was a police operation on 26 April 2005, which effectively curbed a riot at a punk concert in Kirov. Apparently, the police acted on the basis of good intelligence, because a fight involving at least 68 skinheads armed with chains, baseball bats, metal knuckles and metal rods was stopped within minutes.

---

58   It has been reported that other top officials in Russia, including President Putin, received similar "death sentences".

59   For more information on the application of the Law on Combating Extremist Activity see: Verkhovsky A., Kozhevnikova G. "Tri goda protivodeystviya. Tsena nenavisti". (Three Years of Combating Extremism. The Price of Hatred) in *Natsionalizm v Rossii i protivodeystvie rasistskim prestupleniyam* (Nationalism in Russia and Opposition to Racist Crimes). Moscow: SOVA Center 2005. Pp. 111–129.

Unfortunately, effective policing of this sort is an exception, rather than the rule. Incompetent and often illegal law enforcement practices lead to counterproductive outcomes. For example, in St. Petersburg, skinheads caught red-handed and arrested for beating an ethnic Armenian in 2002 avoided punishment due to the expiration of the statute of limitations. However, the police who arrested them were found guilty (and rightfully so) of beating one detainee and sentenced to prison terms.

In an effort to prevent ethnic violence, police and prosecutors in some regions - including Kursk, Ivanovo, and Yekaterinburg - meet with foreign students and advise them on how to keep safe in the streets of Russian cities. However, very often this form of prevention is merely a bureaucratic formality. Thus, for example, in Voronezh, the local police jointly with the department of education produced Safety Guidelines for foreign students focusing mostly on advice to foreign students not to go to certain places at certain times. Sometimes this type of bureaucratic exercise is openly cynical. Also in Voronezh in November 2005, soon after the killing of a Peruvian student, a new position was created in the city administration: the Mayor's advisor on interactions with foreigners. At the same time, the city's graduate schools – where the foreigners study - hosted lectures by the NDPR leader Alexander Sevastyanov.

In St. Petersburg - a city that pioneered the publication of Safety Guidelines for foreign students in 2004 - police blamed foreigners for putting themselves at risk by following the guidelines. For example, the guidelines said, *"if you choose to run, run as fast as you can,"* while in January 2005 a high-ranking police officer in St. Petersburg was quoted as saying that *"by their behavior, foreigners often provoke groups of youngsters to violent offences. Seeing a group of youngsters, foreigners – usually from Asian and African countries – often start to run; by doing so they attract attention and are pursued."*

Equally cynical was a statement published by a number of political leaders during the Moscow City Duma elections, denouncing the Right March. The authors of the statement, including Yuri Luzhkov, Gennady Zyuganov, Sergey Baburin and Vladimir Zhirinovsky, voiced a demand *"to nip in the bud any attempts to put up against each other people of different ethnicity and faith."* Shortly before the statement, Zhirinovsky and Zyuganov refused to denounce members of their parties who had participated in the march. The Moscow City Government headed by Luzhkov failed to impose any administrative sanctions to suppress and punish nationalist pronouncements during the Right March (except removing a few random marchers who carried a swastika) and then banned an anti-fascist march. Baburin by that time had already made his speech to the Union of Russian People congress.

Besides, many officials continue to deny the existence of radical nationalism in Russia, making only general political overtures concerning the need to overcome xenophobia. Regional "tolerance-promoting programs" are little known at best - many of them were adopted without any consultations with civil society. At worst – such as the Krasnodar Territory program – they do nothing to promote tolerance, but make ethnic problems even worse.

3.4. The Fight Against Xenophobia as a Political Resource

We should also describe a new extremely disturbing and notably increasing trend that first appeared in 2005: the use of anti-Nazi and anti-xenophobia slogans as an instrument of suppressing political opposition and independent organizations.

The first part of the trend is not new. Anti-xenophobia slogans have long been used to discredit political opponents outside the country; for example, Latvia and Estonia have been targeted for their rehabilitation of former Waffen SS members. In 2005, the most visible episode of this type was the beating of Russian diplomats' children in Poland and a subsequent beating of Polish nationals in Moscow.

Racist and ethnically motivated attacks are equally disgusting wherever they happen. However, while many attacks against foreigners in Russia may be at least as cruel as the beating of Russians in Poland, the latter elicited an immediate and highly emotional response by Russia's top political leaders, causing tensions in Russian-Polish relations. On the other hand, subsequent attacks against Poles in Russia did not only fail to provoke any political response, but have not been, and probably will never be, investigated. In contrast, in Poland the attackers were promptly arrested. Moreover, a number of Russian media outlets interpreted the beatings of Poles in Moscow almost as "fair revenge" for the attack of Polish skinheads, and openly insisted that "a draw be declared" of the beating match.

Another part of the same trend is excessively tough persecution of fairly harmless leftist youth organizations for the only reason of their opposition to the current political regime. Not limited to excessively severe punishment of NBP members' non-violent protests and to accusing NBP of fascism,[60] persecutions also affect members of AKM, SKM and other leftist groups. An obvious example of them being targeted was the preventive arrest of leftist youths on the eve of the Victory Day, when they were planning a peaceful manifestation.

And finally, the third and most important part of the trend is the use of anti-Nazi rhetoric to discredit political opponents.

The pro-Kremlin Nashi group was the first to move from abstract statements about the "conspiracy against Russia" to concrete political accusations targeting, alongside skinheads and NBP, also Yabloko Party, Committee 2008, Garry Kasparov and Irina Khakamada - i.e. politicians and groups opposing President Putin, but never known for anything like xenophobia. We have reasons to believe that Nashi are behind increasingly common, even systematic street attacks against NBP members and other lefties.

Simultaneously with Nashi, the Federation Council Speaker Sergey Mironov once again voiced his long-cherished idea of amending the Russian Constitution to allow Vladimir Putin to retain his presidency after 2008. Now Mironov argues his case by references to the growing fascist threat in the country.

A ban on the anti-fascist march to be held in Moscow on 27 November in response to the Right March caused a high-profile scandal. The ban was motivated by "inconveniences [likely to be caused] to Muscovites" (the argument could have been valid given that the march was planned on a weekday in Tverskaya street, but we should remember that a march by Nashi in Lenin-

---

60   The NBP ideology, formed in the '90s, closely resembled fascism, according to many experts. Changes in the party's policies over the recent years are not totally convincing, because NBP has not denounced its former statements in any way. Therefore, describing it as part of the democratic opposition - as some observers increasingly do - is premature, in our opinion. However, while some central core and regional activists subscribe to right-wing radical views, they are ultimately forced to leave the party. NBP has never organized violent racist or ethnically motivated attacks; regardless of its aggressive rhetoric, the party is not inclined to violence. Therefore, it is wrong to mention National Bolsheviks next to Nazi skinheads.

sky Prospect in May was not regarded by authorities as an inconvenience). The Moscow City Government permitted a rally in Belorussky Railway Station Square instead of a march, but the organizers declined saying that "it takes a march to oppose another march." Instead, they held an anti-fascist picket in front of the Moscow Mayor's Office on 27 November. The picket was unsanctioned, so the city authorities were legally allowed to break it up. However, the excessive violence of riot police in breaking up a peaceful picket (one participant had to be hospitalized) and the fact that a neo-Nazi rally held by NSO at the same time in Preobrazhenskaya Square in Moscow was not noticed by the city authorities or the police, suggest that the Moscow Government encourages nationalists - whatever the real motives may be.

Another outrageous attack by the government against civil society activists was reported in Nizhniy Novgorod. In 2005, authorities initiated a trial of Stanislav Dmitrievsky, director of the Russian-Chechen Friendship Society. He was charged under article 282 part 2 of the Criminal Code for inciting ethnic hatred, namely, for a publication of statements by Aslan Maskhadov and Akhmed Zakayev. Both statements are, of course, biased and strongly critical of those who hold political power in Russia, but do not contain any sign of ethnic hatred, so there is no reason whatsoever for this kind of charges against the publisher.[61] On 3 February 2006 Dmitrievsky was sentenced to two years of imprisonment but put on probation.

---

61   The statements and the case file materials can be accessed from the website of the Russian-Chechen Information Agency: http://www.ria.hrnnov.ru/modules.php?name=Articles&pa=list_pag&cid=4.

Conclusions

The conclusions that we can make looking back at the year 2005 are less than optimistic.

On a positive side, the Russian authorities increasingly prosecute illegal conduct by right-wing radicals. Apparently, improved sentencing, both in number and in quality, for racist attacks in 2004 - 2005 caused a decrease of hate killings. Possibly, the fact that serious criminal prosecution of racist propaganda started in 2005 will cause a decrease of such offences in the future. However, the government's efforts to combat these offences continue to lag behind the activities of neo-Nazis and other radical ethno-nationalists, especially their promotional and organizing actions. The state is insufficiently systematic and consistent in opposing them, raising doubts about its commitment to eliminating hate crime.

Racist and other neo-Nazi violence is expanding; it becomes increasingly emphatic and affects new ethnic, religious and social groups.

In an attempt to mainstream their ideas, right-wing radicals use all promotional methods available to them. Unfortunately, mass media often present right-wing radicals as independent media personalities and by doing so partially legitimize them in front of the audience.

Apparently, the government still fails to recognize the right-wing radical threat as a top priority, although the electoral successes of Rodina and DPNI with their nationalist rhetoric during the Moscow Duma campaign clearly demonstrated that these are not marginal groups, which you can ignore or easily control through administrative intrigues. Moreover, the clearly political context of pressure on Rodina (as opposed to the LDPR, for example) devalues the state's declarations about fighting xenophobic sentiments; it undermines public confidence in the law and creates a strong belief that political opposition to the regime, rather than right-wing radicalism, is punished.

In fact, in 2005 the problem of xenophobia became a handy instrument of political manipulation used to intimidate democratically oriented electorates, to discredit liberal opposition, to achieve desired electoral outcomes locally and ultimately to perpetuate authoritarian methods of government. Dead set on opposing the mythical "orange threat" and motivated by their own xenophobic attitudes and personal interests, members of political elites preferred to remain passive at best, and collaborate with leaders and ideologists of Russia's right-wing radicalism at worst.

Apparently, the ruling elites in Russia continue to believe that extreme nationalism is not a real political threat; moreover, they seem to believe that "soft" nationalism can be safely and successfully incorporated in the official ideology. Their mistake lies not only in the underestimation of threats other than political – even now, right-wing radicals kill dozens, injure hundreds and poison the minds of many more people with their propaganda. They also underestimate the political threat: extreme nationalism continues to grow, and we have no reasons to believe that the ineffective Russian government can successfully control right-wing radicals should the latter mobilize in the face of a crisis.

III. The 2006 Annual Report

Summary

The year 2006 was marked by substantial developments in the sphere of ethno-religious xenophobia and radical nationalism in Russia. Unfortunately, most of these developments accelerated negative trends of the past, and even caused some new ones to emerge.

Alongside the stable quantitative growth of racist violence (at least 17% as compared to 2005), we observed some qualitative changes, such as the introduction of firearms and explosives, as well as the new demonstrative and explicit nature of such xenophobic crimes.

Public activism of right-wing radical groups was on the rise in 2006. The characteristic features of the past year in this respect included: massive public events; efforts to make a link with social issues and reorient demonstrations into ethno-religious protests; the emergence of new, formerly unthinkable, alliances; and the strengthening and explicit manifestation of links between political groups and skinheads (in particular, some members of the State Duma and regional legislatures openly collaborated with skinheads and offered them direct legal assistance).

Moreover, since the second half of 2006 - i.e. the Kondopoga riots - we have witnessed the active and ubiquitous expansion of ethno-nationalism both in public life (even some politicians formerly regarded as "liberal" used nationalist rhetoric) and in official domestic policies, such as the anti-Georgian discriminatory campaign and the populist ban on foreign traders (commonly understood as "ethnic aliens") selling goods in the Russian retail markets.

The past year also generated some positive developments, such as consolidation of anti-fascist forces; the increasingly active criminal and administrative prosecution of right-wing radicals; the improved legal codification of such offenses; and the emergence of the European Court of Human Rights (ECHR) case law as an instrument useful to adjudicate ultra right-wing activity in Russia. Unfortunately, the achievements in all these areas were weak and more importantly, inconsistent. They failed to slow down – let alone stop – the rapid escalation of xenophobic manifestations.

Moreover, in 2006, the practice of using anti-extremism rhetoric and legislation to discredit and harass political opponents or independent groups and publications not only expanded, but also became an increasingly apparent and permanent feature of domestic policy. At the same time, pseudo-antifascist activities further confused Russian society's already vague conceptions about the unacceptability of public xenophobia.

Unfortunately, our analysis of the 2006 events and phenomena did not reveal any overall improvement of the situation with regard to manifestations of radical nationalism in Russia. Unless consistent, proactive and politically unbiased measures are taken to counteract hate crime and xenophobic propaganda before the federal elections, the situation cannot but deteriorate even further.

1.   Manifestations of Radical Nationalism

1.1.   Violence

The most notable – and, fortunately, still the least acceptable to the public – manifestation of aggressive nationalism was racist and neo-Nazi violence, which, just as in past years, continued its steady growth. As of this writing (March 2007), we know of 563 victims of such attacks, of which 61 lost their lives. These findings show a 21% increase in comparison to 2005 (465 victims, 47 deaths).

Keep in mind that these numbers are known to be underestimated. For example, they do not include attacks against homeless people, even though the law enforcement authorities officially stated in many such incidents that skinheads were behind the attacks (we know of seven such killings and one beating in 2006). Likewise, these statistics do not include victims of massive fights (simply because it was impossible to count the victims), and victims of anti-homosexual attacks during May 2006 attacks in Moscow (on 27 and 28 May 2006 alone skinheads and other homophobes battered at least 50 homosexuals). These stats also do not include victims of "acquisitive" crimes, except those in which the police explicitly found racist motives. Incidentally, the latter have been increasingly recognized by courts, on top of being identified by investigators. For example in 2006, out of the 31 convictions where the racist motive was recognized by courts, at least nine[1] included "acquisitive" charges – it is likely that the offenders increasingly used robbery to conceal the real reason behind the attacks.

In addition to such assaults being more numerous, there are some noticeable qualitative changes.

Firstly, violence by organized skinhead gangs was more open and demonstrative. This explicit nature can take various forms; whereas before it was mainly expressed by claiming responsibility for violence (not to mention vandalism), attacks to mark certain events are now more common (in addition, of course, to skinheads' long-standing tradition of "celebrating" Hitler's birthday on 20 April). Such explicit attacks are particularly common in St. Pe-

---

1   The exact legal qualification of crimes is not always known.

tersburg where diverse skin groups are organized and coordinated better than elsewhere. To give one example, a nine-year-old black girl Lillian Sissoco was assaulted shortly after the end of the trial over the killing of another nine-year-old girl, Khursheda Sultonova. This trend has been gradually spreading to other communities, particularly to Moscow. For example, to commemorate 40 days since the death of Dmitry Borovikov, the leader of an odious skin-group in St. Petersburg, skinheads in Moscow staged a series of attacks, targeting at least seven people.

The attackers sometimes demonstrate that they are not afraid to be stopped. They commit crimes in broad daylight, in public places and/or in front of surveillance cameras. For example, skinhead assailants blatantly killed young Armenian Vigen Abramyants on the platform of Pushkinskaya Metro Station on 22 April 2006.

The explicit manner of neo-Nazi offenses was obviously designed to attract media attention and to promote skinhead groups from marginality and criminality to the public sphere. Skin group leaders aspired to reach the level of popular media figures represented in print and broadcast media alongside the so-called respectable politicians. Their strategy worked. Starting in the spring of 2006, mass media – particularly TV – coverage of the problem of racist violence, combined with some journalists' lack of professional skills, created a situation in which skinheads were allowed to participate as equals in the debate on the growth of xenophobia in the country. Videos of racist violence formerly published on banned or scarcely ever visited websites, were broadcast all over the country without anything to balance the impact - such as reports of trials and sentences meted out to racists.[2] The apogee of skinhead campaigning was the NTV program on 30 December 2006 featuring a 15-minute film about Russian right-wing radicals, which can only be interpreted as a neo-Nazi promotional film.[3]

---

2   See an overview of skinhead violence in: Galina Kozhevnikova. Skinheads on TV. *Natsionalizm i ksenofobiya*. SOVA Center.15 May 2006 (http://xeno.sova-center.ru/213716E/21728E3/7502623).

3   Same Author. "Analiz rezul'tatov monitoringa yazyka vrazhdy v rossiyskikh SMI (sentyabr' – dekabr' 2006)" (Hate Speech Monitoring in the Russian Media: a Review of Findings (September - December 2006)). Presentation at the conference "*Yazyk vrazhdy i ksenofobiya: Rossiya, XXI vek*" (Hate Speech and Xenophobia:

The objective of penetrating mass media - which had been set by neo-Nazi activists in earlier years - was met over and above, so that Dmitry Dyomushkin's Slavic Union abandoned website hacking, a tactic earlier seen as a cheap and safe method of self-promotion. They did not need it any more; D. Dyomushkin, just like other neo-Nazi activists, gained access to a much more powerful instrument of promotion – the Russian TV.

Secondly, in 2006, the nature of violence also changed. Skinheads used guns and explosives instead of bare fists and knives. The most serious damage was caused by the explosion in Cherkizovo market in Moscow on 21 August 2006. There, a handmade bomb in the market killed 13 people, including two young children, and wounded 53.[4] Admittedly, there had been other incidents of Nazi crimes involving firearms and explosives in the past (such as a series of antisemitic posters wired to explosive devices in 2002, the attempted assassination of Anatoly Chubais, and the blast attack against a Grozny-Moscow train on 12 June 2005). But these acts had been either manifestations of "interpersonal" xenophobia (sometimes combined with common banditry[5]) or terrorist attacks committed by mature adults, veterans of local wars and conflicts of the '90s. Additionally, usually these were one-time occurrences. Now, terrorist suspects are young people who have not served in the army, but who are closely linked to law enforcement authorities - although indirectly (the suspects include children of high-ranking police officers, students of police academies, etc.), and to the so-called "military patriotic" clubs. Plus, they are suspected of *systematic*, rather than one-time, terrorist activities ("the Cherkizovo bombers" are suspected of at least nine blasts).

The activity of right-wing controlled, "military patriotic" clubs has increased, rather than decreased, despite the investigation into the SPAS club, where the leader was one of the suspected Cherkizovo bombers. In addition to ideological conditioning, young members of such clubs are trained in contact fighting and the use of firearms and explosives. Taking advantage of the

---

Russia, 21st Century"; Moscow, 8 February 2007. The presentation will be published in full in a book to be produced by SOVA Center in May 2007.

4   11 people were killed immediately, and two more died within a month.

5   Three persons were convicted in 2006 for planting a bomb under an antisemitic poster in Tomsk in 2002. They were charged under 11 criminal articles in total.

popular rhetoric of national insularity and militarism, right-wing radicals enjoy the United Russia Party endorsement in the creation of such clubs. In light of the above, we can expect further, and quite possibly dramatic, escalation of right-wing terror.

The new methods and means of racist violence are accompanied by substantial changes in the membership of such groups. New phenomena have emerged from inside the skinhead subculture populated mostly by teen-agers. They no longer leave skinhead gangs, as they grow older. It was very unusual in the past to see a 20-year-old skinhead, but now it is quite com-mon. Moreover, as older members come back from penitentiaries (also a re-cent development), their prison experience is transferred to other members of the gangs. The above-mentioned "military-athletic clubs" transform isolated and undisciplined local teen gangs into prototype Storm troopers, which the "adult" ultra-right seem to be ready to rely on. As the skinhead movement "matures," its members' educational and social status improves, facilitating access to schools, contacts with law enforcement, and financial and legal support from the ultra-right. All these developments have not been fully real-ized, but they are increasingly manifested.

And finally, racial violence by single-handed attackers is more common than in the past. The case of Alexander Koptsev - perpetrator of a stab attack on 11 January, 2006, in a Moscow synagogue, injuring nine people - though thankfully not killing anyone - is just one odious, high profile case, but it is by no means unique. On 25 June in Novosibirsk a man armed with a hunting rifle spent an hour shooting at people whom he judged by their appearance to be from the Caucasus. We increasingly hear reports of nationalist violence caused by the so-called "Chechen syndrome" where Chechen war veterans attacked people with non-Slav appearance and explained their aggression by saying that *"our guys lost their lives in Chechnya, and now we need to get square with all 'blacks."*[6] This occurred on 12 June 2006 in Kaliningrad, where a series of attacks perpetrated by employees of a private security agency af-fected ten migrant workers from the Central Asia. The fact that such incidents

---

6   Igor Orekhov. "Gasterbayterov izbivali beysbol'nymi bitami" (Migrant Workers Were Beaten with Baseball Bats). *Komsomol'skaya Pravda*, Kaliningrad, 14 June 2006 (http://kaliningrad.kp.ru/2006/06/14/doc120833/).

have multiplied indicates an expansion and heightening "intensity" of xenophobic propaganda, thereby inciting mentally unstable individuals to commit violent crimes.

1.2. Vandalism

Vandalism is a traditional manifestation of xenophobic and neo-Nazi aggression. Vandalism commonly affects religious buildings and installations. It is important to note that no religious denomination or faith is immune.

In 2006, at least 70 acts of vandalism were reported in Russia[7] where religious hatred was the main motive (out of the total 96 in which we found to be motivated by neo-Nazi or xenophobic attitudes). As was the case with the above incidents of violence, this estimate is very conservative and takes into account only those episodes in which the hate motive was evident (selective targeting, offensive graffiti, no valuables stolen, etc.).

Jewish organizations are particularly targeted by such attacks, with over half incidents of vandalism (36) – a major increase since the previous year, when we documented 27 acts of vandalism against Jewish facilities. In Volgograd, a security guard was injured in an attack against a Jewish school. Three attacks – in Surgut (Tyumen Region), Khabarovsk and Astrakhan – were combined with arson attempts.

Attacks against Orthodox Christian installations came second with 12 incidents, which is a substantial drop as compared to the previous year, which had 30 incidents of anti-Orthodox vandalism. As opposed to other faiths, Orthodox Christian sites are not targeted by skinheads, but mainly by those who call themselves "Satanists." They destroy crosses in cemeteries and cover installations with offensive graffiti, "Number of the Beast" etc. Neo-Pagan skinheads also target Orthodox sites. In 2006, there were two such cases – one in Yelabuga, where a swastika was painted on the wall of the Spas Cathedral, and one in Rybinsk, where skinheads covered the walls of a local museum housed in a former Orthodox monastery with offensive graffiti.

---

7   The numbers are different from those quoted in the paper by A. Verkhovsky and O. Sibireva are due to the fact that not all incidents of vandalism were related to religious intolerance.

The third on the list of targets are Muslim religious installations,[8] attacked by vandals 11 times, including two incidents (in Yaroslavl and in Vladimir) of Molotov cocktail bombs thrown at mosques, and a strong blast outside a mosque in Yakhroma, a town near Moscow. The latter is suspected to involve the Slav Union, its leader D. Dyomushkin and the "Cherkizovo bombers."

Very often, such offenses revealed a complex form of xenophobia. To give an example, anti-Caucasus graffiti was painted on a Protestant church and an Orthodox church was covered with antisemitic slogans. The best-known illustration of the latter combination is the "antisemitic" theory of the fire in the Troitsky (Trinity) Cathedral in St. Petersburg (featuring six-pointed stars on its domes). The fire broke out on 25 August. According to representatives of the Orthodox eparchy, they had received several threatening phone calls in August, with the callers specifically mentioning the stars, while after the fire, the cathedral was visited by *"bulky, aggressive looking young men"* who asked the staff whether it had occurred to them that the fire might have been their *"punishment for restoring six-pointed stars on the domes."*

We documented at least 8 acts of vandalism motivated by the neo-Nazi ideology, including desecration of memorials to World War II victims and anti-fascist memorials (for example, in Pushkin, in a suburb of St. Petersburg, offensive graffiti was painted over a monument to Ernest Telman). Some attacks targeted the offices of "ideological" opponents, as in Ukhta (Komi), where the city committee of the Communist Party came under attack in January, or in Samara, where the headquarters of the Union of Communist Youth was targeted in March.

Similarly to the racist violence, vandalism is increasingly overt and explicit. A series of attacks may occur over a few days (e.g. the Yaroslavl mosque was vandalized twice over one week, and the Ulyanovsk synagogue was targeted twice over three days) or vandals may show off (by acting in broad daylight, watched by witnesses or surveillance cameras). For example, it is known that at least twice neo-Nazi vandals targeted buildings located next to FSB offices (in Vladivostok and Rybinsk, Yaroslavl Region).

---

8   Without the North Caucasus.

1.3. Spontaneous Mass Conflicts

The highest-profile mass conflict with a distinct nationalist flavor was reported in Kondopoga, Karelia, in early September 2006, but this conflict - which we will cover below - was by far not the only one in the past year. In the spring of 2006, a pogrom targeting ethnic Azerbaijani villagers occurred in Kharagun, Chita Region, In this incident, a drunken fight escalated into massive riots against ethnic Azerbaijanis living in the community, killing one and injuring at least four. In addition, a few cars and eight houses owned by ethnic Azerbaijanis were set on fire. Regional media reported that all Azerbaijanis left the village following the events.

The second conflict occurred in June 2006 in Salsk, a city in Rostov Region where, fortunately, the disturbances stopped short of pogroms. A quarrel between two young men - an ethnic Russian and an ethnic "Dagestani" - led to a series of apparently criminal clashes, and then to a massive fight involving guns, killing one and injured several people.

As opposed to Kharagun, the latter incident evolved over a relatively long period, so it is obvious that police inaction and failure to interfere in a timely manner allowed the conflict to progress and result in casualties. Angry over the law enforcement inaction, local residents came out for a meeting where, we should emphasize, no nationalist slogans were voiced. Even though anti-Caucasus leaflets were disseminated in the city immediately after the killing, nationalists did not dare to come to the first meeting. After a short time, the Movement against Illegal Immigration (DPNI) led by Alexander Belov (Potkin) and supported by local Cossacks intervened in the Salsk conflict and succeeded in framing the social protest as an interethnic one. However, by the time DPNI intervened, some time had elapsed since the conflict allowing strong emotions to subside. Furthermore, local authorities had made a genuine effort to prevent any further escalation.

And finally, the events in Kondopoga were triggered by drunken behavior of two patrons in a local restaurant (both with a criminal history). A mass fight erupted which involved the restaurant's "krysha" (a Russian word, which literally means "roof". Here it is used as a slang term meaning "protection by organized crime") due to total police inaction. The fighting killed two and heavily injured six; a large part of local residents interpreted it as an "interethnic conflict" leading to many days of pogroms, which targeted people from the Caucasus.

All such conflicts follow the same pattern, which we have described on many occasions: an interpersonal (often "drunken") quarrel understood as an "inter-ethnic conflict"; the inaction of police or local administration; and finally riots. In 2006, however, we observed three distinct types of official responses to such incidents. In Kharagun, the entire conflict was relatively short (it was over in one day); the law enforcement intervened promptly, while the right-wing radicals were not allowed to get involved. All suspected perpetrators were promptly arrested, and subsequent attempts by local national-patriots to seize the initiative and to reinterpret the conflict, in the spirit of DPNI, as *"national liberation struggle of the Russian people against occupants,"* were decisively suppressed by the Region prosecutor's office, which made a public statement specifically for the occasion.

In Salsk, the police eventually intervened, and the suspected killer was arrested almost immediately. DPNI became engaged in the conflict at a later date, after the emotions had cleared - partly because they had been aired during the anti-police meeting. At the same time, authorities made tremendous efforts (it appears that sometimes these efforts were not entirely legal) to suppress any right-wing radical propaganda, to the extent that someone directly involved in the conflict (in fact, the local DPNI leader) was forced to speak on local TV with a conciliatory message to the community.

In Kondopoga, the police procrastinated, the local administration refused to act, while the right-wing radicals engaged in the conflict virtually all at once and coordinated all their steps using the DPNI website. We are aware of the immediate outcome, but long-term consequences of the conflict are not yet obvious – or resolved.

1.4. Activities of Right-Wing Radical Organizations

The last year was marked by the growing activity of ultra-right organizations, particularly, as before, the Movement against Illegal Immigration (DPNI). However, alongside and in close association with DPNI, other right-wing radicals were increasingly active and often made public appearances as a fairly sustainable coalition – DPNI, the Russian All-National Union (RONS), the National Imperial Party of Russia (NDPR), the Slavic Union (SS), and the Russian Order. In provinces, similar nationalist actions, while invariably involving DPNI, also engaged local activists from Rodina, Narodnaya Volya, the Union of Russian People, and some local national-patriotic groups.

1.4.1. Mass Actions and Riots

The two biggest successes of the right-wing radicals in 2006 were the homophobic campaign in April and March and the mentioned events in Kondopoga. Incidentally, the former was also a rare case where DPNI was not the leading group in the campaign.

The homophobic campaign was related to the widely advertised gay festival planned in May and which was expected to feature the first-ever Gay Pride March in Russia on 27 May. In early and late May, two waves of homophobic violence swept across Russia, including violent assaults against homosexuals, attacks against gay clubs, etc. The police conduct on the night of the 1 May (the beginning of anti-gay riots) effectively encouraged the homophobes: instead of controlling the aggressive, but small, mob surrounding the gay club where the festival was planned, police only kept the mob off the entrance to the club (but did not protect the patrons coming in), and then escorted everybody out of the club. On the following days police actions were adequate (maybe even too harsh), but they failed to stop the homophobes. The assailants took advantage of this license (notably, one of the clubs was burned down in these days). Token administrative fines imposed on some detained attackers (instead of criminal prosecution for violent assaults) also strengthened the sense of impunity in the right-wing radicals and failed to deter them from further violence. Suffice it to say that the detained attackers included at least one of suspected Cherkizovo market bombers.[9]

Given the high level of homophobia in the Russian society, a harsh reaction by anti-homosexual activists was predictable, but no one expected that their protests would grow into open and organized violence. We should note here the key role played by RONS leader Igor Artyomov, who led and coordi-

---

9   Which may be the reason behind the prompt announcement by investigators in Moscow that RONS was involved in the Cherkizovo bombing.

nated the homophobic actions.[10] However, the massive attack against the Gay Pride marchers on 27 May involved a diversity of nationalist activists. To reiterate, the May events around the Gay Pride were one of the most successful actions undertaken by right-wing radicals in 2006 and in the previous years. By picking an issue likely to attract media attention and relying on widespread homophobia in society, RONS with its partners gained maximum possible exposure. Moreover, they secured endorsement of the riots by a part of Russian society, which would have never supported racist violence of the same type. These right-wing radicals garnered the vocal support of those people who generally disapproved of their other activity (such as the Union of Communist Youth (SKM) activists or singer Yuri Shevchuk).

In addition, the organization of their action in Moscow was the first and a fairly successful lesson in the open coordination of violent attacks over the Internet, and the first (and so far, the only one) lesson in joining efforts with other forces - skinheads and Orthodox fundamentalists, with whom they had had no contacts before.

Another major success of the right-wing radicals was the mentioned events in Kondopoga. Admittedly, their success was short-lived, because following the riots in Karelia, the "nationalist initiative" was snatched from the ultra-right by the government.[11] However, in terms of publicity and program goals (i.e. to promote and legitimize ethno-nationalist, discriminatory practices), the right-wing radicals won a victory in Kondopoga. Admittedly, these radicals could not organize such riots themselves, lacking the means and resources. But they were mobile and used an effective campaigning strategy. The right-wing radical activity in Kondopoga was the culmination of DPNI's prior experience in organizing diverse actions (including failures as well as successes). They showed their ability to engage promptly (within 24 hours) in a local conflict, to coordinate their efforts over the internet, to organize a promotional campaign on the web and in mass media, to stage "support actions" in other Russian regions, and to campaign effectively in the streets (DPNI produced and distributed Kondopoga stickers in less than one day!) - and to do all of the above simultaneously.

---

10   See details in: G. Kozhevnikova. Spring 2006: "Skin-piar-kampaniya" (Skinhead P.R. Campaign). *Natsionalizm i ksenofobiya*. SOVA Center. 28 June 2006 (http://xeno.sova-center.ru/29481C8/78A0D48#r8).

But on the other hand, the success achieved in Kondopoga had a downside for DPNI and their leader. Upon his return from Karelia, A. Belov appeared to have thrown all caution to the wind. In an attempt to repeat their Kondopoga success and to take advantage of the public hysteria skillfully fueled by adept use of mass media, he organized a serious of explicit provocations – ranging from a right-wing radical student rally in Moscow to announcing a Russian March in the Moscow Metro. These actions undermined his reputation with skinhead groups (DPNI's key supporters), and also placed him in a position of confrontation with the government, which had never been the case before.

In addition – and we reiterate – the authorities were worried over the Kondopoga events and effectively snatched the nationalist initiative from the right-wing radicals. The latter found themselves in direct competition with government for the xenophobic sentiments of the Russian public, which should be seen as part of campaigning for the forthcoming elections. Therefore, DPNI (as competitors, rather than a destructive, unlawful group) came under increased law enforcement pressure. In particular, A. Belov, among others, faced prosecution for incitement to ethnic hatred in a criminal investigation launched by the prosecutorial office of Karelia into the Kondopoga events.

Nevertheless, since November 2005, DPNI, newly encouraged by the scale and resonance of the neo-Nazi march in Moscow, attempted nearly every month to organize various meetings and pickets. Mostly using social slogans (such as protests against illegal drugs, against the installation of a monument to Geidar Aliev in Moscow, etc.), the organization claimed each time that the action was expected to equal the Russian March in its scale. But they never succeeded in attracting more than two hundred people. For example, a rally in Oryol "in the memory of General Yermolov" was preceded by heavy promotion and co-organized on 24 May by four groups - DPNI, Narodnaya Volya, RONS, and the Union of Russian People, but failed to attract a substantial number of marchers, even though it featured Belov and a number of activists coming in from other cities.

---

11   See the section: Expansion of Nationalism into Public Life.

On 4 November 2006, they failed to attract as many people as the year before: their meeting in Devichye Field gathered around a thousand people, but only if we count Baburin's supporters and other national patriots, who kept aside from DPNI, and other right-wing radicals (i.e. even taking into account the preventive arrests of potential marchers, the number of participants was not anywhere near that of the previous year). Admittedly, the success of the 2006 Russian March was not determined by the number of people attending the meeting in Moscow, but rather by the fact that similar marches were held in 13 Russian cities (and in three other cities where they had been unlawfully suppressed by police). In fact, various nationalist-patriotic groups had attempted, on a number of occasions, to hold coordinated public events across the entire Russian territory, but in recent years they were not able to organize any noticeable meetings in more than three regions at once.[12] The geographic spread of the 2006 Russian March suggests that right-wing radicals are shifting their attention from Moscow to provinces.

The right-wing radicals have abandoned the idea of constructing their "parties" from the top down and have adopted a more realistic (proto) party-building approach – well-coordinated, systematic, and diversified both in geographic reach and content: from legal support of convicted "comrades-in-arms" in prisons to assistance to orphanages. Last year's march, as the first public event on a national scale organized by the ultra-right in recent years, was the culmination of their organizing efforts. Admittedly, the xenophobic subtext of National Unity Day – immediately accepted by the Russian ultra-right as "their holiday" - played a certain role. However, another nation-wide public action "in defense of political prisoners" held in early 2007 showed that a convenient holiday is just one factor of success, among others.

1.4.2. Political Maneuvers of the Right–Wing Radicals

The organizational life of the right-wing groups in 2006 was rather uneventful. Arguably, the most notable development was the formation of the National-Bolshevik Front (NBF) by National Bolsheviks who shared right-wing

---

12   For a description of such an attempt see, for example, G. Kozhevnikova. "*Radikal'nyy natsionalizm v Rossii: proyavleniya i protivodeystvie*" (Radical nationalism in

radical (at times explicitly Nazi) views and who had left Eduard Limonov's party (the main target of government-endorsed "anti-fascism") for ideological reasons.[13] The NBF founding conference was held in Moscow on 29 August - a symbolic date marking an anniversary of a cruel attack against National-Bolshevik Party (NBP)[14] activists the year before. Members of the pro-Kremlin party *Nashi* were believed to be behind the attacks. As soon as the NBF was announced, its members immediately declared that they were forming a coali-tion with Alexander Dugin's Eurasian Youth Union (ESM). The front and the coalition declared their common goal of "combating the orange threat" in sup-port of the current government. The fact that the National Bolshevik ultra-right came back to Dugin appears logical, given that Dugin was the originator of those ideas and diatribes, which caused some observers to consider National Bolsheviks a fascist party. It is widely known that members of the ESM who declare loyalty to, and enjoy favors from, the current government were the official organizers of the 4 November 2005 Right March in Moscow. These members also committed a series of violent attacks against various oppo-nents, which they do not even attempt to hide, but rather tend to publicize them as much as possible. So we are observing a paradox, characteristic of the "state-sponsored anti-fascism" in Russia: Limonov's NBP, increasingly left-wing and openly oppositional, is labeled "fascist" by the official propa-ganda, while the actual right-wing radicals of BNF and ESM have abandoned their oppositional views and can now claim government support.

The first half of 2006 was also marked by attempts of the right-wing radicals (DPNI and their allies) to establish closer links with the Communist Party by taking advantage of all mass meetings organized or attended by Communists, such as protests against the housing reform, celebrations of

---

Russia: Manifestations and Responses). Price of Hatred. Moscow: SOVA Center, 2005. pp. 11–12.

13   Interestingly, virtually all ex-National Bolsheviks convicted under article 282 of the Criminal Code over the past two years joined NBF.

14   The attack targeted activists of several leftist groups, such as NBP, AKM, SKM, Un-ion of Youth for Fatherland. However, only National-Bolsheviks were hospitalized, and it is unclear whether and how many members of other groups had been af-fected as well. See details in: "Napadenie na natsbolov v Moskve" (Attack against National-Bolsheviks in Moscow). SOVA Center. *"Demokratiya v osade"* (Democracy under Siege). 30 August 2005.

"Soviet" holidays - 23 February, 1 May - meetings in the memory of Serbian ex-President Slobodan Milosevic, etc. Initially, right-wing radicals simply joined meetings and marches - and the Communist organizers did not object, unlike in 2005. Later, the right-wing members were accepted as full participants to the extent that some CPRF meetings featured A. Belov as an official speaker.

However, there was no noticeable follow-up, and in the second half of 2006 DPNI sought a closer relationship with Dmitry Rogozin, resulting in "revival" of the Union of Russian Communities (KRO) on 9 December 2006.[15] (A. Belov joined the Presidium and the Central Council of KRO as *"the KRO Council leader for propaganda"*).

Other events in the organizational sphere included a congress held on 27 November by the Union of Russian People, a coalition of Orthodox-monarchist groups formed in November 2005. The congress sought to overcome the differences, which had brought the organization to the verge of splitting up since the death of its leader sculptor Vyacheslav Klykov in early June 2006. Formally, they were able to reconcile and elected General Leonid Ivashov from the Military-Imperial Union to SRN Chairman. But internal conflicts continue to paralyze the organization.

On 16 December 2006, the Russian National Unity announced the establishment of a new movement named after Alexander Barkashov. It made no real difference: the part of RNE led by Barkashov remains in crisis, while each RNE group independent from Barkashov acts on its own.

Certain nationalist MPs of the State Duma are more active and, importantly, more explicit than before about their collaboration with the ultra-right groups. We should mention Nikolay Kuryanovich in the first place - who is effectively "a pocket State Duma member" for the neo-Nazi groups and assists them with his parliamentary enquiries which he uses to pressure investigators on cases against hate promoters and skinheads accused of violent crimes. His MP status allows him to voice ultra-right slogans and get away with it, as well

---

15   Interestingly, at least one person charged with an offense under article 282 has been included in the Congress' governing body. Either KRO founders are confident of what the outcomes of the criminal proceedings will be, or they knowingly provide a justification for an eventual ban (denial of registration) under the anti-extremism law, later to be presented as political repression.

as to organize nationalist events, etc. He was ousted from the Liberal Democratic Party on the eve of the Russian March, leaving him no chance of being re-elected. But N. Kuryanovich, in addition to being a member of DPNI, is also a member of the Orthodox fundamentalist Union of Orthodox Gonfalon-carriers (UOG) and a member of the Central Council of the neo-Nazi SS (giving up his position in KRO leadership).

In 2006, more State Duma members openly demonstrated their links with right-wing radicals. Victor Cherepkov (Baburin's Rodina Party) did not only take part in the right-wing radical meeting on 23 February 2006, but also, as neo-Nazis claimed, hired an SS skinhead as his assistant. In January 2006 it was revealed that S. Baburin himself joined the Union of Russian People founded two months before. MP Sergei Ivanov of the LDPR openly collaborates with the National-Socialist Society. Andrei Savelyev, the ideologist of Rogozin's Rodina, officially joined DPNI in 2006.

To reiterate, the links between members of the Duma and neo-Nazis had always been known, but before 2006 they had not been demonstrated so explicitly. The current situation shows that the boundaries of what is permitted in the Russian politics are expanding.

The same is evidenced by the maneuvers around the Russian March. Firstly, the preparation for the event, which was perceived as a neo-Nazi march from the start (as seen from the publicized membership of the Organizing Committee, which included SS leader D. Dyomushkin), involved at least seven Duma members.[16] Secondly, MP Sergei Baburin enabled the neo-Nazis to hold their "march" legally by obtaining permission for his own party to hold a public meeting and allowing DPNI and skinheads, as well as Makashov and supporters of Colonel Kvachkov (charged with attempted assassination of Anatoly Chubais) to participate. The important thing is not that Baburin, a relatively moderate politician, dares to collaborate openly with right-wing radicals - it is not unusual - but that he (like Victor Alksnis who is not an ethno-nationalist at all) is prepared to collaborate even with explicitly neo-Nazi groups.

---

16 Five members from Rodina Party (D. Rogozin, A. Savelyev, V. Alksnis, I. Savelyeva, and B. Vinogradov) and two from the LDPR (N. Kuryanovich and I. Musatov).

So we have been observing a change of configuration in the potential alliances of right-wing radicals in comparison to the previous decade.

1.5. Nationalism and Xenophobia as an Electoral Resource

Even though the electoral process is heavily regulated, nationalist slogans and provocations are still actively used in election campaigns, both as "negative publicity" and as a way to attract voters.

So, for example, during additional elections to the State Duma from Medvedkovsky Electoral District No 196 in Moscow, held on 12 March 2006, there were three ultra-right candidates – Colonel Vladimir Kvachkov, *Russkaya Pravda* paper founder and publisher Alexander Aratov and political writer Igor Dyakov know for his neo-Nazi views. The first two were under criminal investigation at the time. Even though the three had no chance of being elected,[17] they promoted right-wing radical propaganda under the cover of election campaigning (Kvachkov's campaigners, for example, were arrested by police for disseminating SRN brochures which had nothing to do with the candidate).[18]

Nikolai Kuryanovich was involved in the election campaign of LDPR MP Alexei Mitrofanov for the position of the Mayor of Dzerzhinsk, a city outside Moscow. Speaking at a campaign meeting, he advocated a residential policy favoring *"an ethnically clean community."*

In contrast, candidate to Saratov city legislature Andrei Palaznik from United Russia, to the best of our knowledge, did not voice any nationalist slogans of his own, but he made Ilya Lazarenko, a veteran of the Russian right-

---

17   Meaning not only that A. Aratov and I. Dyakov had negligible chances of winning the elections, but also the Election Committee's obvious and widely expected bias against Vladimir Kvachkov, who closely missed being elected to the State Duma in the additional elections in December 2005. After Kvachkov became the only candidate successfully competing with the United Russia candidate, virtually no one doubted that he would be given no other chance of running for elections. See: Election Committee denies Col. Kvachkov registration for elections. SOVA Center. *"Natsionalizm i ksenofobiya v Rossii"* (Nationalism and Xenophobia in Russia). 2 February 2006 (http://xeno.sova-center.ru/45A2A1E/6CB10D9).

18   None of the three reached the final stage of the elections, but they took advantage, albeit not fully, of the publicity offered by the campaign.

wing radical movement,[19] head of his election campaign headquarters. A few days after the elections, the law enforcement authorities in Saratov announced that they had *"prevented a serious nationalist provocation"* which, they asserted, Lazarenko had been preparing on the eve of elections.

In addition, it is interesting to note the way nationalist rhetoric is used in election campaigning indirectly, by reference to past scandals still on the public mind. For example, Sergei Lektorovich, a well-known and rather popular nationalist in Samara, who used to be the local Rodina Party leader for a while when he ran (unsuccessfully) for the mayor of Samara, used a promotional poster featuring his own photo and a slogan "Let Us Clean Samara from Trash», closely associated with Rodina's scandalous promotional video entitled "Let Us Clean Our City from Trash." On 12 March 2006, Alexander Kuzmin was elected mayor of Megion, a city in Khanty-Mansiysky Autonomous District after three unsuccessful attempts; in 2005, he was accused of nationalist propaganda and of bribing the voters and banned from campaigning just one day before the second tour of elections. We are not sure whether Kuzmin used nationalist slogans in 2006. But it is certain that even before his first election campaign he had been known to most local residents for his nationalist slogans – it was only in this context that this candidate was discussed on local web forums in 2005.

We can see in both cases - Lektorovich, and to a lesser extent, Kuzmin – that they referred in their campaigning to the same nationalist manifestations, which had been officially repressed earlier. The cases of Kuzmin and the Moscow Rodina Party – i.e. candidates removed from elections for nationalism - are extremely rare in the Russian electoral practice.[20] Reference to these past cases, on the one hand, was self-explanatory, and on the other hand, tapped into public discontent with the government's authoritarian practices.

---

19   See details on Lazarenko, see A. Verkhovsky, *"Religioznyy faktor v parlamentskoy kampanii 1999 g."* (The factor of religion in the 1999 parliamentary election campaign). Moscow: Panorama Center, 2000 (http://www.panorama.ru/works/patr/bp/7rus.html).

20   See G. Kozhevnikova. "Osen'-2006: Pod flagom Kondopogi" (Autumn 2006: Under the Kondopoga Banner). *Natsionalizm i ksenofobiya v Rossii.* SOVA Center. 4 January 2007 (http://xeno.sova-center.ru/29481C8/883BB9D).

1.6. Expansion of Nationalism into Public Life

The year 2006 revealed an inconsistency between the anti-xenophobic rhetoric of government officials and actual government practices. On the one hand, officials at various levels – from President Putin to governors and mayors – and also pro-governmental political parties and organizations have declared so often that xenophobia and racial intolerance must be suppressed, that these declarations are perceived as well-polished clichés.

But on the other hand, the government officials and pro-governmental figures rarely set a good example in this respect. Since 2006, questionable statements, initiatives and contacts of the so-called respectable politicians and statespersons have been increasingly reported. For example, in May, a transcript was published of the April meeting held by the parliamentary party Council, St. Petersburg Legislative Assembly; it featured openly nationalist pronouncements not only by LDPR members, but also by United Russia MPs.

Admittedly, some events can be explained by mere ignorance. It is unlikely that the United Russia Party knowingly provided a gym for Slav Union training (as D. Dyomushkin said on REN-TV). It is more likely that they had thought some "military-patriotic club" would use the space. But more frequently, their contacts with, or endorsement of, nationalists appear to be a conscious choice. So, for example, we can hardly assume that the Moscow city government was unaware of the fact that the mentioned A. Aratov faced civil and criminal proceedings for propaganda of racial and religious hate content The participation of his *Russkaya Pravda* with its racist and antisemitic publications in the Moscow International Book Fair had provoked scandals more than once. However, this history did not prevent A. Aratov and his publishing company from winning a Moscow government-sponsored mass media award twice within two months.

The Russian Football Union (RFU)[21] and its conduct in 2006 are also worth mentioning. In early 2006 football season, RFU joined the FIFA agreement providing for serious punishment of football clubs for racism should it manifest in their own practices and their fans' behavior. *"FIFA requires that a*

---

21   Technically, RFU is an NGO, but in reality it is closely linked to the government.

team be stripped of six points for racist manifestations. All our clubs have been warned, and I cannot rule out that we may apply such measures," said RFU President Vitaly Mutko at the time. But no clubs were punished during the 2006 season, even though all Russian tournaments are known to take place in a racist atmosphere, and in the summer of 2006 an international scandal broke out over an interview given by Locomotive player Stefan-Andre Bikey of Cameroon to a UK paper; he said that he was planning to leave Russia because of continuous racist manifestations. But neither this, nor the Nazi flags in the stadiums, nor even the records of fans' racist behavior in the game reports[22] triggered any real measures by RFU.

On the other hand, there is a persistent tendency to deny the problem and dismiss the demands to investigate racist crimes as some "political agenda." This tendency is particularly noticeable in St. Petersburg. In the spring of 2006 the city prosecutor Sergey Zaitsev (maybe the only high-ranking government official in Petersburg who had previously admitted a systemic problem of racism in the city), Mikhail Vanichkin (at that time the head of the City Department of Interior),[23] and Tatiana Linyova (chair of the Governor's Human Rights Commission) used virtually the same language to declare that increased attention to St. Petersburg due to a series of outrageous racist attacks was nothing more than "provocation against the city." Eventually, Governor Valentina Matvyenko, commenting on the arrests of racist suspects, made a reference to "threads leading to Moscow."

Following the events in Kondopoga, efforts to legitimize xenophobic (particularly anti-migrant) rhetoric and discriminatory practices became a mainstream trend in domestic politics.

Initially, it was voiced by regional officials and public figures. Karelian Governor Sergey Katanandov responded to the Kondopoga events with statements comparing the characteristics of "us (our people)" and "them" - apparently, forgetting that all people involved in the conflict were Russian citizens. In Chechnya, Ramzan Kadyrov immediately responded, saying that he would protect "his people" in Karelia, and by doing so both high-ranking offi-

---

22   We are not sure whether the fans' racist behavior had ever been recorded in football game protocols before the 2006 season, but the Russian media covering sports reported them as being unprecedented in the history of Russian football.

cials assumed the roles of tribal chiefs. Head of Murmansk Department of Interior Valery Zvontsov offered his recipe of "inter-ethnic harmony": *"... adopt legislation establishing quotas: 30 percent of places in the market may be held by Azeri, and 70 percent must belong to locals."* This kind of statements inevitably triggered a massive anti-migrant campaign under the slogan of "cleansing the marketplace from non-Russian traders," especially made possible since the Russian President spoke on 5 October about protecting the interests of *"indigenous Russian population"* in retail markets. Of course, the President meant Russian citizens (rather than ethnic Russians), but his entire statement was structured in such a way that many people, and not only right-wing radicals, interpreted it as an expression of solidarity with the DPNI rhetoric.

Following this presidential statement (it was not "a slip of the tongue," because the President repeated it on two occasions), a massive campaign of discrimination was unleashed, including a Decree issued by the federal Government in December which banned foreigners from certain roles in retail trade starting on 1 April 2007. Chronologically, these events were a follow-up of the fizzling anti-Georgian campaign – the first incident of officially endorsed ethnic discrimination in contemporary Russia. The campaign targeted ethnic Georgians with Russian passports, as well as citizens of Georgia. Ethnic discrimination campaigns had occurred in Russia before on many occasions (particularly those targeting Chechens after major terrorist attacks), but they had never been publicized. This time, however, TV outlets and part of the print media establishment were directly involved in racist propaganda.[24]

This official policy was picked up and carried on by pro-governmental political groups, who adopted both the right-wing radical practices and their rhetoric. So, in end-November 2006 the Movement of Young Political Ecologists of the Moscow Region – the Locals (a regional clone of Nashi) undertook a series of "anti-migrant" actions virtually identical to those organized or proposed by DPNI, such as unwarranted patrolling of the streets, ID checks,

---

23   In August 2006 he was appointed Assistant Minister of Interior.
24   G. Kozhevnikova's presentation at the conference "*Yazyk vrazhdy ...*" (Hate Speech
      ...).

stopping people of certain ethnicity, and provocation to fighting.[25] As opposed to DPNI, the Locals did not risk being suppressed by police (administrative arrests of a few activists did not make much difference).

All of the above suggest that the "nationalist initiative" - methods as well as slogans – is increasingly shifting to government and pro-governmental structures in anticipation of elections (not only the future federal elections, but also regional elections, as was the case with the Locals in Moscow region, where the elections were held on 11 March 2007).

It has been obvious since Kondopoga that the liberals lack a uniform position concerning "acceptable boundaries of xenophobia." For example, the leadership of Garry Kasparov's United Civic Front (UCF) failed to respond to their Karelia chapter, which effectively expressed solidarity with the Kondopoga rioters by commending their actions as a "*manifestation of civic self-government.*" Even Garry Kasparov himself did not see any problems last spring with having one of Russia's infamous ultra-right figures - Andrei Savelyev - speak as a guest at the first UCF conference.

Yabloko Party leadership failed to dissociate themselves from the nationalist election campaigning of their Krasnoyarsk leader Vladimir Abrosimov; likewise, there was no reaction (except Sergei Ivanenko's promise to "sort it out") to Aleksei Navalny of Moscow Yabloko saying that he did not denounce any of the Russian March slogans.

---

25   Let us remind the reader that the same principle (patrolling retail markets, pickets in front of traders' stalls urging customers not to buy from "non-Russians," etc.) was used by right-wing radicals to promote Rodina on Moscow City Duma election in 2005.

2.   Counteractions to Radical Nationalism

2.1. NGO Activities and Spontaneous Opposition

2.1.1. NGO Activity and Non-Violent Public Counteraction
In addition to traditional implementation of educational, awareness-raising, information and research projects aimed at counteracting xenophobia, Russian NGOs increasingly have realized the need for consolidation of all forces interested in counteracting xenophobia, and the importance of maximum publicity of public initiatives and events. Probably, this awareness came in the end of 2005 following the Right March, when an anti-fascist march was organized in Moscow on 18 December 2005.

In 2006, this work continued. On May 14, 2006, a conference was held in Moscow entitled *Fascism is a Threat to Russia's Future* and was attended by more than 150 representatives of NGOs, youth associations, democratically-oriented political parties, informal anti-fascist groups, national-cultural associations, experts, journalists, and workers of culture. The participants adopted a Program of Action to guide the Russian Anti-Fascist Front (RAF) founded on 22 June in Moscow.

RAF's first major public event was an anti-fascist meeting held on 4 November 2006 jointly with the Left-wing Anti-Fascist Front (LAF)[26] in Bolotnaya Square in Moscow and attended by approximately 800 people. The organizers reached what we believe to be a fundamentally important agreement banning the use of any party symbols during the non-partisan event (and also giving up the official Russian three-color flag at LAF's insistence).[27] A group of neo-Nazis had planned to attack the meeting, but the police blocked their access to Bolotnaya Square and then stopped their activists.

Mass events were held in other Russian cities as well. We should mention the traditional March Against Hatred held in October in St. Petersburg in the memory of anti-fascist researcher Nikolai Girenko (in 2006, the march at-

---

26   A coalition of the left-wing activists and their sympathizers united under anti-fascist slogans (see the coalition's manifesto at http://laf.drugoi.com/manifesto/), established in the summer of 2006.

27   It was the use of party and organizational symbols that caused serious conflicts among the Anti-Fascist March participants on 18 December 2005.

tracted 500 participants), and the Patchwork of Peace[28] organized by the Perm' Memorial chapter as part of the City Day celebration on 12 June, attracting a few thousand people.

The anti-Georgian campaign in the autumn of 2006 triggered active public protests, from meetings in Moscow to individuals changing their last names to Georgian names, to the *I am a Georgian* web-based campaign, etc.

Spontaneous protests against the government's failure to counteract racist violence continued. Even though racist violence is a fact of everyday life in Russia, the law enforcement agencies rarely recognize racist motives of crimes; therefore only vigorous public protests give any hope of changing the investigators' attitudes. For example, on the night of 24 to 25 April, members of the Armenian Diaspora blocked the traffic at the crossing of the Garden Ring and the New Arbat in Moscow, protesting against the investigators' denial of racist motives in the murder of a young Armenian in the Moscow Metro. The Prosecutor's Office in Moscow insisted, against comprehensive evidence, that it was a mere interpersonal conflict. In St. Petersburg in autumn, soon after the killing of an Indian student, foreign undergraduate students held a meeting and demanded that the authorities protect them from neo-Nazis.

2.1.2. Activities of Left-Wing Radicals and Antifa

In 2006, anti-fascist activities of more or less radical left-wing groups, previously noticed only by social researchers, came strongly into the public focus.

SKM, AKM, and other youth organizations made a number of statements in spring protesting against collaboration between CPRF and DPNI. We note the absence of response to these protests by the Communist leaders; however, there was no continuation of their attempts at collaboration.[29]

But the lefties did not limit themselves to statements, and on 1 May, right in front of the State Duma building, a fight occurred between skinheads trying to join the Communists at a rally, and anti-fascist leftist youth who

---

28   The quilt panel made of 20 by 20 cm squares was 2 meters wide and more than 120 meters long.

would not let them do so. It was just one of the first episodes of the street war between right-wing and left-wing radicals. Of course, more or less violent clashes between these youth groups had been reported before, but most of them had not come into the public eye before 2006.

The lefties had usually been targeted alongside various youth subcultures seen by Nazi skinheads as enemies (including the "red" skinheads). Counter-attacks had been rare. The situation changed as new groups emerged, bringing together members of diverse political and non-political movements around their common goal of counteracting Nazi skinheads. Such groups are usually termed "antifa" – and they often use this term to describe themselves. Not unexpectedly, some such groups opt for violence as the main method of "re-educating" the neo-Nazi. We will call them "militant antifa" - as opposed to those who do not accept violence as a method of protest.

The opposition between "militant antifa" and neo-Nazis was particularly felt in the autumn of 2006, when two peaceful meetings of right-wing radicals were attacked: the attackers targeted the audience of a music concert organized by right-wing radical groups and the participants of an "anti-Caucasus" meeting outside Oktyabrskaya Metro Station in Moscow on 14 September, and then a DPNI meeting in St. Petersburg on 17 September.

The anti-fascists explained their attacks by the government inaction and failure to respond to the neo-Nazi threat, but the violent acts committed by anti-fascists are as illegal as similar actions of their opponents, not to mention that usually random bystanders are also victimized by such attacks. In addition, attacks by militant antifa do not seem to suppress the right-wing radical activity: on the contrary, they provoke further escalation of the street war between Nazi skinheads and militant antifa, and thus more neo-Nazi terror. For example, in December 2006 in Moscow there was an attempt at the life of a young antifascist (an explosive was planted outside his apartment, and 5 police officers were injured as it was defused).

Of course, radical anti-fascists ("militant" as well as all others) also employ other methods of fighting neo-Nazi, such as rallies, stickers on the walls,

---

29   Following the spring events, CPRF and DPNI have not organized any joint actions that we know of.

painting over neo-Nazi graffiti, and fairly effective (even though illegal) hack attacks.

2.1.3. The Public Chamber

In describing public efforts to counteract nationalism, we should mention the activities of the Public Chamber formed in late 2005. The most significant of its undertakings was the adoption of anti-extremist recommendations by its first plenary on 14 April 2006; the recommendations had been prepared by Vladimir Tishkov, the Chamber's Chair of the Commission on Tolerance and Freedom of Conscience. These otherwise reasonable recommendations had one important, built-in defect: they were based on the excessively broad legal definition of extremism stipulated in relevant legislation. The final draft, which in the process of editing had lost some of what we believe to be important recommendations (in particular, the recommendation to eliminate an ethnocentric approach in teaching history and social sciences), was published in the summer of 2006, but we are not sure if there has been any follow-up.

As to the Public Chamber's other vocal statements against radical nationalism, they hardly merit a positive assessment. Some of them certainly demonstrated an active position of the Chamber members as citizens, but at the same time revealed an obvious lack of expertise concerning the issues in question. On the other hand, continuous public statements allegedly made on behalf of "the public" and which urged even tougher anti-extremist policies, such as V. Tishkov's suggestion that mass media should be punished for nationalist citations, effectively supported unlawful restrictions of civil liberties under the pretext of fighting extremism (see below).

We should also note that certain members of the Public Chamber do not practice what they preach. For example, Pavel Gussev, editor-in-chief of *Moscovsky Komsomolets* daily and chairman of the Public Chamber Commission for Communications, Information Policies and Media Freedom of Expression, repeatedly urged media to be tolerant in 2006 and even initiated an appeal to his colleagues in May to banish from print and broadcast publications *"political adventurers and promoters of racial, ethnic, religious animosity, hatred and violence.*[30] His daily, however, is one of the most xenophobic periodicals in Russia, known for explicitly racist reporting.

2.2. Cases Brought before the European Court of Human Rights

In December 2006, the European Court of Human Rights considered two applications related to xenophobia in Russia. Both judgments appear very significant.

On 12 December, ECHR rejected an application brought by RONS leader I. Artyomov in 2005 after Russian courts at all levels denied RONS official registration as a political party, because their name contained the words "Russian national." I. Artyomov alleged in his application to the European Court that by denying his group registration, the Russian Ministry of Justice violated Article 11 of the European Convention of Human Rights (right to freedom of association). However, the European Court found that RONS intended to defend the rights of only one ethnicity - ethnic Russians, which was inconsistent with *"the guarantee of equality... [and] the fair treatment of minorities in the political process."* The Court also found that this type of discrimination *"requires from the authorities special vigilance and a vigorous reaction."*

Two days later, on 14 December, ECHR considered an application filed by the chief editor of Gorodskye Vesty (Volgograd) Anatoly Karman. In September 1994, A. Karman published an article describing a high-profile local right-wing radical, chief editor of the Volgograd *Kolokol* paper Stanislav Terentyev as "a local neo-fascist"; Terentyev filed a defamation suit, which he finally won after years of litigation in 2001. Failing in all his appeals, A. Karman took the case to Strasbourg, and ECHR found the Russian authorities to be in violation of Article 10 of the Convention (freedom of expression). The court awarded the journalist 1,000 euros in compensation to be paid out by Russia. We believe this to be a landmark judgment, because the vagueness of terms such as "fascism" and "fascist," among others, in contemporary Russian lan-

---

30   "Glavnye redaktory prizvali sebya k tolerantnosti" (Chief editors called upon themselves to be tolerant). SOVA Center. *Natsionalizm i ksenofobiya v Rossii.* (National-

guage usage has contributed to many defamation suits by right-wing radicals against Russian journalists and human rights defenders. There is no possibility of predicting the outcome of such litigation, but whenever the plaintiffs win, it serves to legitimize right-wing radical propaganda.

2.3. Criminal Prosecution of the Right-Wing Radicals

A review of criminal prosecution targeting right-wing radical nationalism and xenophobia reveals some positive progress in this area, even though serious negative attributes persist.

2.3.1. Violence

In many instances we observed positive progress in the criminal prosecution of racist violence.

Firstly, we saw the substantial numerical growth of guilty verdicts and convictions for violent crimes where the hate motive was recognized. We also observed that the number of such convictions doubled each year: in 2003, there were 4 convictions, in 2004 – 9; in 2005 – 17, and in 2006 - 33 convictions. Last year, more than 100 persons were convicted for violent racist attacks (as opposed to 55 convictions in 2005). Unfortunately, the number of convictions failed to catch up with the number of crimes, but some communities have reported local progress. According to regional civil society activists, skinhead activity in Voronezh substantially decreased following a series of anti-racist verdicts.

The geographic distribution of convictions for racist violence has expanded, covering 17 regions of the Russian Federation (see Table 4), while our review of these trends has revealed time and again that lack of judicial practice is the main reason why investigators and judges fail to address the hate motive. The successful completion of a few investigations and trials could set an important precedent for the further adjudication of hate crime and racist violence. Just a few successful trials serve to establish the new approach. At the same time, the sad fact is that the impressive growth of the number of con-

ism   and   Xenophobia   in   Russia),   5   May   2006   (http://xeno.sova-center.ru/213716E/21398CB/743062F).

victions has occurred in the provinces, rather than in Moscow and St. Petersburg where most skinhead attacks take place.

The proportion between (a) criminal convictions where the hate motive is recognized as an aggravating circumstance and (b) convictions under article 282 (essentially punishing for "hate propaganda") has not changed since 2005 (in 15 of the 33 convictions, the hate motive was recognized as an aggravating circumstance, while at least 14 convictions for hate crimes where under article 282; to compare, in 2005 six out of the 17 convictions addressed the hate motive as an aggravating circumstance, and eight convictions were under article 282[31]).

Nevertheless, we observed a certain general improvement in the legal qualification of such offenses. For example, in 2006 we documented the first known case where the hate motive was mentioned as an aggravating circumstance (to note - it is applicable to any criminal offense) under article 63.1.e by the Prosecutor's Office in Voronezh Region in the trial over the murder of a Peruvian student; one defendant faced murder charges, and the others faced charges under article 63 for hooliganism and robbery, aggravated by racist hatred. Even though the court did not support these charges, the attempt in and of itself was important.

In addition, racist motives are increasingly recognized in cases involving "acquisitive" offenses – to reiterate, at least nine of the 31 convictions for hate-motivated crimes in 2006 included charges of robbery. Moreover, in the spring of 2006, following the arrests of the Borovikov-Voevodin group, the Prosecutor's Office in St. Petersburg did something unprecedented: they officially recognized that the group robbed post offices to support their neo-Nazi activity.

Authorities have gradually adopted the practice of prosecuting rightwing radicals for the organizing of extremist communities (article 282[1] of the Criminal Code). In 2006, there were three or four sentences under this article (as opposed to two in 2005) in St. Petersburg (against the Mad Crowd leader Ruslan Melnik[32]), in Belgorod (the Roma family case) and in Verkhnaya Py-

---

31 We are not aware of the legal qualification in four other cases.

32 However, we believe this sentence was passed in addition to the previous sentence against the same group passed a year earlier, in December 2005. See: Extremist

shma, Sverdlovsk region. In the last case, though, the judgment was inconsistent. The court found the three defendants guilty of setting up and being involved in an extremist community (a prosecutorial press release said they had set up a community *"for committing hate-motivated crimes against people from the Caucasus and Central Asia"*). The three defendants were at the same time found guilty of murdering a Kyrgyz in January 2005, and two of them were already convicted in December 2005 for an overtly racist murder of three Armenians. However, the judges failed to recognize hate motives in each of the two murders. Does it mean that they set up an extremist community *"for committing hate-motivated crimes"* – but the actual crimes they committed were not motivated by ethnic hatred?

Similarly, we believe it to be a positive development that a number of neo-Nazi ideological violence cases found their way to court, including an attack against a young female anti-fascist in Yekaterinburg, and a riot at a punk concert in Kursk. The current criminal legislation does not allow for adding a hate motive to the charges faced by the perpetrators in these cases. But it is of special importance for us that the law enforcement authorities recognized the neo-Nazi ideology behind these crimes.

Admittedly, the tendency of denying nationalist motives persists. We note however, that reports of prosecutors finding explicitly neo-Nazi attacks to be "mere hooliganism" are less common than before. The real reason may be under-reporting, rather than absence of such cases. In 2006, we know of five convictions where prosecutors failed to find racist motives. In one such case - in Togliatti (Samara Region) - the racist motive was recognized in official statements made by local prosecutors, but was not included in the formal charges. Also of interest was another trial, ending in February 2006, over perpetrators of an attack against an imam in Sergyev Posad. Even though the perpetrators were yelling anti-Islamic slogans during the attack, even though anti-Islamic leaflets were disseminated in the city on the eve of the trial, even though racist insulting remarks to witnesses and victims were made in the courtroom, the offense was qualified as mere hooliganism. The best-known scandal of this type

---

Mad Crowd group members sentenced. *Natsionalizm i ksenofobiya*. SOVA Center. 14 December 2005 (http://xeno.sova-center.ru/45A2A1E/687D980); Mad Crowd

was the above-mentioned investigation into the murder of young Armenian Vigen Abramyants in Pushkinskaya Metro Station in Moscow. Regardless of numerous eyewitness testimonies, the investigators initially denied the racist motive of the crime; they even arrested a young man who confessed having killed Abramyants following a conflict "over a girl." Some blogs reported massive police pressure on witnesses to force them to withdraw their original testimonies confirming a skinhead attack. It took vigorous public protests to force the investigators to abandon the "personal conflict" theory.

We should also note the persistent tendency towards sentencing to probation terms for such offenses. At least 24 of the 109 perpetrators found guilty of racist offenses got away without punishment or were released on probation or amnestied.[33] Two others were sentenced to short prison terms covered entirely by their pre-trial detention. Some sentences are nothing short of shocking – for example, in Kostroma, four skinheads who physically assaulted five people within two days, got away with conditional sentences.

Speaking about the prosecution for ultra-right-wing violence, we should mention St. Petersburg and Moscow separately.

Firstly, each hardly shows any positive progress in terms of successful trials of such cases (see Table 4). Moreover, in 2006, St. Petersburg acquired the reputation of a city "where jury courts acquit fascists." Indeed, three jury trials (over the murders of Khursheda Sultonova, Roland Epossak, and Wu An Tuan) ended in acquittals. Of course, these cases raised many issues - in particular, due to the high level of organization and information among local neo-Nazi, safety issues plagued jurors and their families. We would argue, however that the primary factor in all these cases was poor investigation, which failed to collect sufficient evidence and convince the jurors that the specific suspects had committed the crimes. Unfortunately, these verdicts revived the debates over removing such cases from the jury courts' jurisdiction and over the feasibility of jury courts in Russia. Notably, these debates bordered closely on propaganda, where opponents of jury courts insisted on "general xenophobia"

---

leader sentenced in St. Petersburg. Ibid., 5 December 2006 (http://xeno.sova-center.ru/45A2A1E/85D177E).

33   Incidentally, some of the skinheads convicted earlier must have been released in an amnesty carried out in May 2006 to mark 100 years of the State Duma, but we are not sure how many of them were released.

shared by all jurors and, as a consequence, argued that anti-racist trials will fail in jury courts. Neither of the above allegations is true. Firstly, we have only observed acquittals by jury courts in St. Petersburg, while in some other cases – including Moscow, Saratov, Volgograd, Vladivostok, and also St. Petersburg – jury trials ended in convictions of racist offenders. Secondly, even in the St. Petersburg trials ending in acquittals, jurors recognized the racist nature of some offenses, so we can hardly support allegations of jurors' xenophobia.

In 2006 in Moscow, the number of convictions slightly increased vs. previous years, but importantly, four out of the five were high-profile trials - the Koptsev case, the attacks against singer Lisa Umarova, media reporter Elkham Mirzoyev and Minister of Culture Zaur Tutov of Kabardino-Balkaria. As an important disclaimer, we do not mean that any high-profile trial is wrong. But it is hard to imagine that the only people targeted by racist violence in Moscow are public figures who can afford a good lawyer. It means that the law-enforcement authorities in Moscow are not particularly active in investigating hate crimes.

We should mention still another trial of right-wing radicals - notable for being the first and only known conviction for making threats against the court and jurors on behalf of a right-wing radical organization. RNE had threatened judges, prosecutors and jurors involved in a trial of two police officers, Vyacheslav Blokhin and Alexei Konovalenko of Dolgoprudny, who were charged with abuse of power.[34] In 2006, it was determined that the authors of threatening letters were ex-member of RNE Yuri Kovalyov and his acquaintance Alexander Matasov. The latter is now on a federal list of wanted suspects, while Yu. Kovalyov was tried by the Moscow City Court in October 2006, found guilty of pressuring a court, and sentenced under several criminal counts to 6 years of settlement colony.

---

34   See details of the Blokhin-Konovalenko case in: G. Kozhevnikova. "*Radikal'nyy natsionalizm v Rossii i protivodeystvie emu v 2005 godu*" (Radical Nationalism and Efforts to Counteract It in 2005). *Natsionalizm i ksenofobiya*. SOVA Center, 6 February 2006.

2.3.2. Propaganda and Campaigning

We have been observing continuous progress in counteracting racist violence, but it is for the first time that we have noted substantial developments in suppressing right-wing radical propaganda.

Just as is the case with the prosecution of racist violence, we have observed a somewhat higher rate of criminal convictions, 17[35] in 2006 vs. 12 in 2005. However important the rate of convictions may be, we believe that even more important is the improved practice of handing out punishments.

Firstly, the convicted campaigners get away without punishment less often than before. Previously, either the statute of limitations would expire by the time of sentencing, or the campaigner would be amnestied, or else a probation sentence would be meted out without any additional penalties. But by the end of 2006 the situation began to gradually improve. (Seven out of 20 convicted offenders got away without punishment - notably, four of the six trials ended in the first half of 2006. In contrast, in 2005 five out of 15 convicted offenders got away without any punishment).

Secondly, courts have increasingly applied punishments other than imprisonment (fines, correctional labor) (8 sentences out of 16). In one case, the court banned the offenders from practicing their profession (sentences to National Bolsheviks, authors of *Para-Bellum* paper in Chelyabinsk).[36]
Thirdly, for the first time since the adoption of the anti-extremism law, judicial precedents have been used to prosecute hate promoters. We know of three such cases in 2006.

In November 2006 in Makhachkala a criminal investigation file against local NDPR activist Andrei Boikov was taken to court; the prosecution was based on a prior judgment finding one of Boikov's texts extremist in 2004.

We believe that the most appropriate and consistent of all such cases was the prosecution of RNE activists in Tatarstan – one of the few Russian regions where following the adoption of anti-extremist legislation, RNE was

---

35   We do not count the sentence for Stanislav Dmitrievsky, which we find unfair.
36   Banning an offender from practicing his profession was also used in the Boris Stomakhin case; unfortunately, these were the only two cases where ban on profession was applied in 2006.

liquidated as an extremist organization, rather than closed on technical grounds.[37]

Firstly, based on the prior judicial ban, the Prosecutor's Office in Kazan charged RNE activists under article 282[2] (participation in a community found by court to be extremist). It was the first instance that we know of in Russia in which this criminal article was used against someone other than Hizb ut-Tahrir Islamic activists. Secondly, reference to the same judgment (which the right-wing radicals had not appealed) was used to convince the Canadian hosting provider of the RNE website to deny services to the group.

At the same time, we note that we are not aware of any sentences in 2006 for xenophobic vandalism in cemeteries (article 244.2.b). Admittedly, such sentences have been extremely rare in previous years as well.

As far as prosecution of hate campaigners is concerned, we need to note a significant political aspect in certain cases, even though the prosecution may not be entirely unfounded (see below). Here we would mention the verdict against Boris Stomakhin in Moscow.

We certainly believe that charges brought against B. Stomakhin were legitimate. But the cruelty of his punishment is shocking — Stomakhin was sentenced under article 282 part 1 and 280 part 2 to five years in prison and a three-year ban on journalism. As of today, it is the toughest sentence under articles 282 and 280 (without reference to other articles) in the entire post-Soviet period. For the sake of comparison, one of the most odious ideologists of contemporary Russian neo-Nazism Yuri Belyaev, who published a *Street Terror How-To* on his website with detailed guidelines on how to organize, carry out and camouflage neo-Nazi attacks, got away with a probation sentence and continues his campaigning.

What made Stomakhin different from most other radical propagandists was his unconditional support of the Chechen separatists, extreme antagonism to the current political regime, and published derogatory comments on ethnic Russians. Apparently, these reasons were behind his sentence standing out from among similar cases. The public opinion overwhelmingly interpreted it as selective enforcement and political bias of the court.

---

37   The Tatarstan Supreme Court ruling of 21 May 2003.

This interpretation was further supported by the context of Stomakhin's conviction and sentence. A couple of weeks before the judgment, the law enforcement authorities in Moscow did not find sufficient reasons to launch a criminal investigation into neo-Nazi calls to violence against a number of high-profile Russian human rights defenders, whose photos and home addresses they published on the Web. At the same time, the Moscow Prosecutor's Office refused to open a criminal case against the neo-Nazi Slavic Union, failing to find anything illegal about it.

2.4. Other Measures of Counteraction

Alongside criminal prosecution, other administrative practices of suppressing right-wing radicals have improved. We cautiously note that, just as it is with criminal prosecution, these improvements are not yet systemic or consistent and, apparently, are due to subjective factors (in particular, professionalism and attitudes of certain officials).

We should mention in particular the Federal Service for Supervision over Compliance in the Sphere of Mass Communications and for Protection of Cultural Heritage, (often referred to as RosOkhranKul'tura) active in suppressing extremist propaganda in mass media. They issued a total of 29 warnings in 2006, which were not challenged in court. We find five of these warnings unfounded, including two warnings triggered by the use of the swastika symbol to illustrate apparently anti-fascist articles. However, outside these cases, we appreciate the fact that RosOkhranKul'tura is much more active in this area now than before. There is hope now that their activity may bring about some positive results: following repeated warnings issued to papers *Duel* (Yuri Muchin) and *Korpus* (National Socialist Society), RosOkhranKul'tura initiated liquidation proceedings against the papers, while the *Russkoye Delo* paper closed voluntarily after a series of warnings.

Similarly, prosecutors' offices increasingly issue warnings to media and other organizations, but prosecutorial practices are not as open to the public as those of RosOkhranKul'tura, and therefore more difficult to assess. In March 2007, an amazing figure was published – prosecutors issued 311 warnings for extremist activity to mass media in 2006. However, we cannot analyze this figure, because in most cases it is unclear who was warned by prosecutors, when and why.

For the first time in two years (since the spring of 2004), three organizations were liquidated for their activity, rather than on merely technical grounds.

In March, a court in Kabardino-Balkaria satisfied a prosecutorial request and liquidated a group calling itself the State Council of Balkaria for "gross violations of effective laws." However, the court refused to find the group extremist, even though the prosecutor's office urged the court to do so.

Two other cases of judicial liquidation occurred in Krasnodar Territory.

In May, following numerous prosecutorial warnings a court found extremist and ethno-nationalist, and then liquidated a group called *The Kuban Rada of Spiritual Ancestral Russian Empire* - a regional chapter of the right-wing radical neo-Pagan Spiritual Ancestral Russian Empire which had announced its independence from the Russian Federation.

In October, the use of swastikas, Roman salute and racist provisions of Slavic-Arian Vedas as elements of a religious doctrine triggered liquidation of neo-Heathen VEK RA group. Notably, the prosecutor's office, again, referred to the 2004 Omsk Region Court judgment banning a similar organization, which also used the Slavic-Arian Vedas as part of its religious teachings.

Administrative sanctions for public use of Nazi symbols, unfortunately, remain virtually non-existent, even though there have been some noteworthy cases. In particular, in June in Novorossiysk local right-wing radical Sergey Putintsev was fined for distributing a newspaper with a swastika-like symbol, while the entire print-run of the paper was confiscated following a court order.

Law enforcement practices aimed at preventing organized violence and right-wing radical propaganda have noticeably improved.

We can quote an example of an efficient police response in Zhukovka, Bryansk region, where a small (around 20 people) anti-migrant rally was organized by DPNI with official permission on 6 July; most participants were local skinheads, who formed a column after the formal end of the rally and attempted to march down the street flashing a Nazi salute and chanting xenophobic slogans. Such manifestations are rarely suppressed in Russia, but in this case they triggered legitimate administrative arrests by police escorting the event. Moreover, later the press office of the Bryansk Region Department of

Interior published a press release with a detailed explanation of the police conduct.

Unfortunately, police often use excessive violence in suppressing nationalist actions - which eventually hinders the criminal and administrative prosecution of right-wing radicals. For example, in June in Syktyvkar, OMON prevented a riot in the city retail market, but used excessive force in detaining the radical nationalists who had been led to the market by Yuri Yekishev (then facing trial). Their use of excessive force was challenged by Yu. Yekishev and his supporters in court, and as a result they were released from administrative arrest and made an (unsuccessful) attempt to sue the OMON officers.

Unfortunately, the efforts to prevent right-wing radical manifestations are not consistent and as such are not making any real difference. We can quote as an example a situation, which occurred in the right-wing radical segment of the Russian web in early 2006. Alexander Koptsev's high-profile attack against a synagogue, apparently triggered by his reading of antisemitic publications on the web, caused prosecutorial offices to declare their commitment to fighting such materials in the Internet. They even arrested two authors of web-based hate publications - in Kaliningrad and Astrakhan Region (the latter, Igor Mogilyov, was later convicted). These prosecutorial declarations and arrests threw the ultra-right in a state of panic. Some of the ugliest materials were removed from websites, forums were either closed or carefully filtered out offensive posts, etc. By mid-March, however, the prosecutorial campaign dwindled, the panic subsided, and some of the resources were restored to their original form and content.

3.   Excessive and Unfounded Actions Against Extremism

3.1.   Legislation

The attack against worshippers in a Moscow synagogue on 11 January 2006 reinvigorated the discussion about the need to strengthen anti-extremist legislation in Russia, mostly by making punishments even tougher. Experts, however, have repeatedly pointed to the fact that the problem is not that the punishments are too mild, but that some provisions are poorly worded and some others are hardly ever enforced.

The first material outcome produced by the debates was a draft law tabled by the State Duma Committee on Civil, Commercial and Procedural Law. The draft – published in late January 2006 - contained many poorly designed provisions and apparently had never been really intended for adoption by the Duma. It was followed by another draft, narrower in scope, and also tabled by the Government, but seeking to toughen and diversify criminal and administrative penalties for vandalism motivated by nationalist, religious and ideological hatred, and also for the manufacturing and dissemination of Nazi symbols.[38] Even though the draft law passed two readings in the Duma by early 2007, the amendments, apparently, are not seen as an urgent matter, and may still be revised. Another, more fundamental lawmaking initiative was launched in the Duma by a group of deputies from different parties – usually indicating Kremlin support – in June.

On 28 June 2006, a draft law amending articles 1 and 15 of the Federal Law against Extremism was launched in the Duma and adopted at a record speed - within one month. It made the already vague definition of extremism even vaguer and introduced liability for "justifying" extremism. The amended law enabled persecution of NGOs whose protests involve any clashes with authorities (violence against officials, threats of violence, and hindrances to the operation of government establishments are now labeled extremism - regard-

---

38   See an overview of threats to democratic liberties contained in this draft law in Lev Levinson's comments on anti-extremist amendments of the Criminal Code and the Code of Administrative Offenses. *Natsionalizm i ksenofobiya.* SOVA Center. 23 January 2007 (http://www.xeno.sova-center.ru/45A2A39/89DD983).

less of the official and the situation), and persecution of any mass media, which publish supportive reports or comments with regard to such protests. The above draft was followed immediately by amendments to the federal law on Main Guarantees of Electoral Rights and the Right to Participate in a Referendum, and to the Civil Code. Under the new amendments, a candidate or a list of candidates may be denied registration, or their current registration may be annulled, should they be found to have engaged in extremist activities. Moreover, candidates may be punished for their alleged extremism retroactively, because the amended law allows looking into their past activities over a period equal to their prospective period in office, if elected. The amendments will not be applied retroactively. However, starting in January 2007, any act potentially interpreted as extremist (and we will explain below that possibilities for such interpretation are extremely broad) may deny someone a possibility of being elected in the future.

3.2. Persecution of NGOs and Civil Society Activists

The enforcement of the newly adopted "extremism" definition followed promptly. As early as the end of August, 2006, it was applied in Bashkortostan to bring charges under article 280.2, of the Criminal Code ("public appeals to the exercise of extremist activity, using mass media") against local opposition journalist Victor Shmakov for his civic activism and organization of public protests against the current Bashkortostan government led by Murtazy Rakhimov. The case was sent to court in December.

Admittedly, the "anti-fascist" measures targeting civil society activists and NGOs continued throughout the year in the framework of the original legislation, whose repressive potential had been revealed at the time of drafting back in 2002.

The highest profile case was that of Stanislav Dmitrievsky and the Russian-Chechen Friendship Society (RCFS), where he was the executive director.

As we mentioned earlier, S. Dmitrievsky was prosecuted in 2005 for publishing statements by Aslan Maskhadov and Akhmed Zakayev in his *Pravo-zaschita* Newspaper. Both statements were, understandably, very critical of Russia's political leadership, but did not contain any ethno-nationalist statements. Initially, authorities attempted to bring charges against the human rights defender under article 280 ("calls for extremist activity"), but later - apparently, seeing no chances of winning the case - they revised the charges, so the case reached the court as "incitement to ethnic hatred" (article 282). On 3 February 2006, S. Dmitrievsky was sentenced to two years of probation. The Supreme Court eventually upheld the verdict.

The NGO came under severe official pressure at the same time as criminal charges were brought against Dmitrievsky; most of these attacks against the group were unlawful and unfounded. However, as soon as Dmitrievsky was convicted, authorities had a formal reason to liquidate RCFS for "extremism." In October 2006, the prosecutor's office filed a liquidation request against RCFS; they referred to the former judgment finding S. Dmitrievsky guilty of an "extremist" offense and to the fact that the group failed to remove him from the list of founders (as required by the amended Law on NGOs) and also failed to condemn him in public (as required by the Law on Combating Extremist Activity). Just two sessions (12 and 13 October) was enough for the court to order liquidation; in 2007, the Supreme Court upheld the judgment.

Similarly, a trial against high priest of ethnic Mari heathen faith and well-known opposition leader Victor Tanakov resulted in a criminal conviction; the prosecutor's office found incitement to ethnic hatred – without sufficient reason, we believe – in his brochure *The Priest Speaks*. On 25 December he was sentenced under Article 282 of the Criminal Code to 120 hours of correctional labor.

Other provisions against extremism have also been used as instruments of pressure on human rights defenders. On 26 February 2006, the Moscow Prosecutor's Office warned the Memorial Human Rights Center for publishing on its website a comment by mufti Nafigulla Ashirov on four Hizb ut-Tahrir books. Mufti Ashirov's text said that the four books (and not the organization's overall ideology) do not call to violence and do not incite hatred against people of other faiths. The comment did not contain a single direct citation from the books, nor did the author express solidarity with them. However, the prosecutors found that it indirectly promoted Hizb ut-Tahrir ideas and "*can be considered propaganda from the point of view of social psychol-*

ogy." Memorial challenged the warning in court, but the challenge was rejected.

3.3. Pressure on Mass Media

The main episodes in which anti-extremist legislation was arbitrarily used against mass media in 2006 were related to the "cartoon scandal" in Russia (a follow-up of the Muslim protests against the publication of the Danish cartoons depicting Prophet Mohammad). While in Europe, the "cartoon scandal" triggered broad public debates concerning the freedom of expression and its boundaries, in Russia at least five media outlets were chastised, including one that had nothing whatsoever to do with the Danish cartoons.

It all started when the United Russia Party chapter in Volgograd Region disliked a drawing illustrating an article about the so-called Anti-Fascist Pact (part of United Russia campaigning launched in early 2006, see below) being signed in the region. The cartoon depicted, in an explicitly tolerant manner, the founders of world religions watching TV – the TV screen showed two groups of people ready to attack each other - and saying: "This is not what we teach them." United Russia accused the paper of xenophobia and contacted the regional prosecutor's office, which responded with unheard-of promptness by warning the paper within a few hours of the UR complaint. A few days later, the paper was closed by its founder, the municipal administration. The entire scandal was a parody, obvious to everyone, given that the explicitly antisemitic newspaper *Kolokol* has been published in Volgograd for more than a decade, and numerous attempts of the local Jewish community to have it closed had failed so far. A few days later, *Volgogradskye Vesti* was reopened under a different name. This incident remains one of the most outrageous and ridiculous examples of arbitrary "anti-extremism."

Certain media outlets have, indeed, reprinted the Danish cartoons as illustrations to relevant discussion. In March, *RosOkhranKul'tura* warned two media companies - web-based *Gazeta.ru* and *Nash Bryansk. Subbota* print paper (*Gazeta.ru* challenged the warning in court, but lost).

The most serious episode of the "cartoon war" ended in criminal prosecution against Anna Smirnova, editor-in-chief of *Nash Region Plus* paper in Vologda Region for reprinting the cartoons as an illustration of an article discussing the "cartoon scandal" (the most controversial parts of the drawings were covered, though). In April, the City Court in Vologda found Anna Smirnova guilty under Article 282 of the Criminal Code and sentenced her to a 100,000 ruble fine. Fortunately, in May, the Regional Court acquitted Smirnova; the paper, however, which was independent of the local governor, had been closed by the owner (husband of the editor-in-chief) back in February, before the court verdict.

In Altai, the local RosOkhranKul'tura office sought liquidation of Bankfax web-based news agency for an offensive statement posted on their forum featuring a discussion of the cartoon scandal. The liquidation proceedings were launched without any prior warning, even though the news agency removed the controversial posting from the forum immediately following complaints. Fortunately, RosOkhranKul'tura lost the case as follows from the Supreme Court ruling of 12 September 2006. Similarly, attempts at criminal prosecution of the news agency staff and the author of the posting failed.

On another occasion, *Zyryanskaya Zhizn* paper in Syktyvkar came under attack for a series of neutral reports about the activity of local right-wing radicals led by Yuri Yekishev, who was later convicted and sentenced for incitement to ethnic hatred. The charges also implicated a highly professional interview with Yekishev, which exposed the nationalist demagoguery. The prosecutor's office warned the paper against extremist activity. The publishers lost their funding sources and were forced to close their paper-based version. Currently, authorities are continuing persecution of the web-based publication.

3.4. Antifascist Rhetoric as a Political Resource

Since late January 2006, anti-fascist and anti-xenophobic rhetoric was increasingly used to discredit political opponents of the ruling political party and to suppress democratic freedoms in Russia.

The so-called Anti-Fascist Pact – an agreement among political parties to counteract nationalism, xenophobia and religious strife and initiated by United Russia Party on 26 January 2006 - can be considered the starting point of an "official anti-fascist campaign."

The Pact urged political parties to deny membership to those who openly profess racist and xenophobic beliefs, to deny support to racist candidates in elections, to refrain from participation in public events involving xenophobic agitation, etc. In fact, the United Russia Party's initiatives could have been welcomed, if the Pact had not been discredited at the outset by its initiators, which included the LDPR. United Russia Party failed to condemn the policy of ethnic discrimination pursued by Governor Alexander Tkachyov of Krasnodar Territory; they failed to oppose the anti-Georgian campaign, not to mention some other, lesser known, episodes. The Anti-Fascist Pact obviously targeted the strongest opponents of the 'ruling party' – namely Rodina and the CPRF, which were not allowed to sign the Pact, as opposed to the loyal LDPR (which hit the headlines shortly before the signing, in particular by its racist proposal to adopt a law against mixed marriages between Russian women and foreigners "to protect the gene pool").

The "anti-fascist" rhetoric enabled UR to unleash the above-mentioned "cartoon scandal" in Volgograd and to continue its attempts at discrediting political opponents (in particular, the Other Russia coalition which includes the National Bolsheviks traditionally accused of "fascism"[39]). We should note, however, that the anti-fascist campaign gradually dwindled between the spring and the summer, and after the Kondopoga events the rhetoric changed dramatically. In early 2007, UR proposed a so-called Russian Project.

We also recall a rather funny case of "mutual political anti-fascism" which took place during the election campaign in Primorye. In September, a complaint filed by the local Legislative Assembly MP Leonid Beltukov of United Russia Party caused the regional court to ban the election campaign and revoke the registration of independent candidate Nikolay Markovtsev who had used a "We Will Be in Berlin" WWII poster in his campaigning. In the poster, a Soviet soldier trampled a Nazi helmet carrying the image of a bear – rather than a swastika. This depiction offended plaintiff L. Beltukov who thought the bear was the United Russia Party symbol and interpreted the poster to associate UR with the Nazis.

---

39   We do not insist that NBP has been accused of fascism for no reason at all. Back in the 90-ies, these allegations were well founded, and we cannot say that the transformation experienced by NBP in recent years has totally done away with the neo-fascist heritage of the "old NBP" (which the critics usually refer to), but in general, NBP today can hardly be described as a neo-fascist organization.

In response, Markovtsev explained that he had intentionally replaced a Nazi swastika by a bear – the symbol of Wehrmacht's 3d Armored Division, rather than the United Russia symbol, because public display of swastika on the poster would have violated the Law on Combating Extremist Activity.

The best-known episode of the "anti-fascist" political pressure was a campaign launched in the spring of 2006 against Governor Oleg Chirkunov of Perm' Territory, who by that time was perhaps the only Russian governor who was not a United Russia member. The pretext for the scandal was an incident at the Open Youth Forum held locally under the auspices of the Governor, where a young neo-Nazi introducing himself as NNP and DPNI member spoke in Chirkunov's presence. On the next day, the Governor apologized to the local public for the incident, while the materials of the forum were made available to prosecutors for a review – and we should say that this type of official response is extremely rare in such cases.

Nevertheless, the pro-presidential populist Young Russia and Nashi groups accused the Governor of sponsoring fascists and staged an anti-Governor rally manned by young "nashists" brought to Perm' from other cities for the occasion. The scandal eventually settled, and in September 2006 Oleg Chirkunov headed the United Russia Party list in the regional elections.

Appendices

Crimes and Conviction Statistics

Table 3: Consolidated statistics of racist and neo-Nazi attacks between 2004 and 2007 (by city)[1]

CITY	2004			2005			2006			2007		
	KILLED	*BEATEN, WOUNDED*	*TOTAL VICTIMS*	*KILLED*	*BEATEN, WOUNDED*	*TOTAL VICTIMS*	*KILLED*	*BEATEN, WOUNDED*	*TOTAL VICTIMS*	*KILLED*	*BEATEN, WOUNDED*	*TOTAL VICTIMS*
Moscow	17	62	79	16	179	195	37	219	257	42	209	251
St. Petersburg	9	32	41	4	45	49	6	53	59	9	110	119
Abakan	0	0	0	0	2	2	0	0	0	0	2	2
Arkhangelsk	0	0	0	0	1	1	0	0	0	1	3	4
Astrakhan	0	0	0	0	2	2	0	0	0	0	0	0
Barnaul	0	0	0	0	1	1	2	1	3	4	4	8
Belgorod	0	5	5	0	4	4	0	18	18	0	1	1
Birobidgan	0	0	0	3	0	3	0	0	0	0	0	0
Blagoveschensk	0	2	2	0	7	7	0	1	1	0	0	0
Bryansk	0	0	0	0	1	1	0	1	1	1	2	3
Cheboksary	0	0	0	0	0	0	0	6	6	0	0	0
Chelyabinsk	1	4	5	0	0	0	0	1	1	0	11	11
Chita region	0	0	0	0	0	0	1	0	1	0	3	3
Irkutsk region	3	0	3	2	5	7	0	8	8	1	53	54
Ivanovo	0	1	1	0	0	0	0	0	0	0	4	4
Izhevsk	0	0	0	0	1	1	0	1	1	1	6	7
Kaliningrad	0	1	1	0	2	2	0	11	11	0	1	1

---

1   In alphabetic order, except Moscow and St. Petersburg, as the main centers of racist violence.

157

CITY	2004			2005			2006			2007		
	KILLED	BEATEN, WOUNDED	TOTAL VICTIMS	KILLED	BEATEN, WOUNDED	TOTAL VICTIMS	KILLED	BEATEN, WOUNDED	TOTAL VICTIMS	KILLED	BEATEN, WOUNDED	TOTAL VICTIMS
Kaluga	0	0	0	0	11	11	1	3	4	0	0	0
Kazan	0	0	0	0	0	0	0	8	8	0	0	0
Khabarovsk	0	0	0	0	3	3	0	0	0	0	0	0
Kirov	0	0	0	0	1	1	0	0	0	0	0	0
Kostroma	0	5	5	0	0	0	0	10	10	0	2	2
Krasnodar	2	32	34	1	3	4	0	7	7	0	9	9
Krasnoyarsk	0	0	0	1	1	2	0	3	3	0	3	3
Kurgan	0	0	0	0	6	6	0	0	0	0	0	0
Kursk	0	5	5	0	2	2	0	0	0	0	0	0
Lipetsk	0	1	1	0	3	3	1	0	1	0	3	3
Maikop	0	3	3	0	0	0	0	0	0	0	0	0
Murmansk	0	0	0	0	1	1	0	1	1	0	5	5
Nizhniy Novgorod	1	5	6	4	12	16	0	36	36	1	39	40
Novgorod	0	0	0	0	5	5	0	0	0	0	0	0
Novosibirsk	2	12	14	1	9	10	0	9	9	0	4	4
Omsk Region	0	3	3	0	0	0	1	3	4	1	1	2
Orenburg	0	0	0	0	0	0	1	1	2	1	1	2
Oryol	0	8	8	0	0	0	0	9	9	0	0	0
Perm'	0	1	1	3	2	5	0	0	0	0	3	3
Petrozavodsk	0	0	0	0	2	2	0	0	0	0	0	0
Pskov	0	0	0	0	1	1	0	0	0	0	0	0
Rostov-Don	0	0	0	0	10	10	0	2	2	1	7	8
Ryazan'	0	0	0	0	1	1	0	4	4	0	6	6
Samara	1	3	4	4	5	9	0	2	2	2	9	11
Saratov	1	0	1	0	0	0	4	4	8	0	1	1
Smolensk	0	0	0	0	2	2	0	0	0	0	0	0

CITY	2004			2005			2006			2007		
	KILLED	BEATEN, WOUNDED	TOTAL VICTIMS	KILLED	BEATEN, WOUNDED	TOTAL VICTIMS	KILLED	BEATEN, WOUNDED	TOTAL VICTIMS	KILLED	BEATEN, WOUNDED	TOTAL VICTIMS
Stavropol	0	0	0	0	21	21	0	0	0	0	7	7
Syktyvkar	0	0	0	0	4	4	0	4	4	0	0	0
Tambov	0	3	3	0	6	6	0	0	0	0	0	0
Tomsk region	0	3	3	0	6	6	0	4	4	0	5	5
Tula region	1	0	1	0	3	3	1	2	3	0	0	0
Tver region	0	0	0	0	0	0	0	3	3	0	2	2
Tyumen region	3	1	4	1	0	1	0	15	15	0	0	0
Ufa	0	1	1	0	2	2	0	2	2	0	1	1
Ulan-Ude	0	0	0	0	0	0	0	0	0	1	0	1
Vladimir region	0	4	4	0	0	0	0	0	0	0	5	5
Vladivostok	5	9	14	0	3	3	2	18	20	1	3	4
Volgograd	0	2	2	0	1	1	2	9	11	0	5	5
Vologda	0	0	0	0	0	0	0	1	1	0	0	0
Voronezh	1	2	3	1	21	22	1	6	7	0	15	15
Yakutia	0	0	0	0	0	0	0	0	0	0	2	2
Yaroslavl region	0	0	0	0	0	0	1	6	7	0	2	2
Yekaterinburg	1	7	8	6	6	12	0	6	6	1	16	17
Yoshkar Ola	0	1	1	0	15	15	0	5	5	0	0	0
Yuzh.-Sakhalinsk	1	0	1	0	0	0	0	0	0	0	0	0
Total	49	218	267	47	418	465	61	502	563	68	565	633

Table 4: Consolidated statistics of racist and neo-Nazi attacks in 2004-2007 (by season)

	2004[1]			2005[2]			2006[3]			2007[4]		
	KILLED	BEATEN, WOUN-DED	TOTAL VICTIMS	KILLED	BEATEN, WOUN-DED	TOTAL VICTIMS	KILLED	BEATEN, WOUN-DED	TOTAL VICTIMS	KILLED	BEATEN, WOUN-DED	TOTAL VICTIMS
Winter (Dec. /Jan.+ Febr./ no date[5])	9 (0/ 9/ 0)[6]	25 (0/ 22/ 3)	34 (0/ 31/ 3)	11 (3/ 7/ 1)	74 (14/ 54/ 6)	85 (17/ 60/ 7)	9 (4/ 5/ 0)	113 (57/ 47/ 9)	122 (61/ 52/ 9)	26 (8/ 16/ 2)	175 (50/ 104/ 21)	201 (58/ 120/ 23)
Spring	12	79	91	5	120	125	16	114	130	18	134	152
Summer	16	20	36	7	72	79	18	172	190	12	145	157
Autumn	9	80	89	23	109	132	14	109	123	12	132	144
Year total	49	218	267	47	418	465	61	502	563	68	565	633

1   Besides, we know of *13 killings* of homeless people where the law enforcement authorities suspect an ideological (neo-Nazi) element.

2   Besides, we know of *5 killings and 4 beatings* of homeless people, where the law enforcement authorities suspect an ideological (neo-Nazi) element.

3   Besides, on May 27-28, 2006, in Moscow alone, skinheads and other homophobes battered at least *50 gays.*
The statistics include *13 killed and 53 wounded* by the blast attack in Cherkizovsky Market in Moscow on 21 August 2006.
We also know of *7 murdered and 4 beaten* homeless people, in which cases police suspect neo-Nazi motivation.

4   Except the gays – victims of skinhead attack on 27 May 2007.
We also know of *4 killings* of homeless people where the law enforcement authorities suspect an ideological (neo-Nazi) element.

5   All attacks where we only know the year of the incident are classed under 'January'

6   January-February 2004.

160

Table 5: Consolidated statistics of racist and neo-Nazi attacks in 2004 and 2007 (by the victim of attack)

YEAR	2004		2005		2006		2007	
	KILLED	BEATEN, WOUNDED	KILLED	BEATEN, WOUNDED	KILLED	BEATEN, WOUNDED	KILLED	BEATEN, WOUNDED
Total	49	218	47	418	61	502	68	565
INCLUDING:								
Dark-skinned people	1	33	3	38	2	32	0	35
People from Central Asia	9	23	16	34	13	55	25	69
People from the Caucasus	15	38	12	52	15	72	19	46
People from the Middle East and North Africa	4	12	1	22	0	11	1	16
People from Asia-Pacific Region (China, Vietnam, Mongolia, etc.)	8	29	4	58	4	51	2	43
Other people of "non-Slav appearance"	2	22	3	72	4	68	14	79
Members of youth subcultures and leftist youth	0	4	3	121	3	119	5	192
Others, or not known	10	57	5	21	20	94	2	85

Table 6: Statistics of convictions taking into account the racial hate motive of violent crimes in 2004-2007

	NUMBER OF CONVICTIONS	NUMBER OF OFFENDERS CONVICTED	INCLUDING CONDITIONAL SENTENCES OR RELEASE FROM PUNISHMENT
2004			
Moscow	4	11	unknown
St. Petersburg	2	10	4
Novgorod	1[1]	1	0
Voronezh	1	3	0
Vladimir Region	1	1	1
Total	9	26	5
2005			
Moscow	2	4	0
Moscow region	4	14	0
St. Petersburg	2	10	4[2]
Blagoveschensk	1	4	0
Lipetsk	1[3]	4	0
Murmansk	1	2	1
Perm'	1	1	0
Tambov	1	1	0
Tyumen region	1	5	0
Vladivostok	1	1	0
Volgograd	1	7	0

---

1   For threats to blow up a synagogue.
2   Still another individual was acquitted for lack of evidence.
3   With a judicial determination addressed to the City Administration.

	NUMBER OF CONVICTIONS	NUMBER OF OFFENDERS CONVICTED	INCLUDING CONDITIONAL SENTENCES OR RELEASE FROM PUNISHMENT
Yekaterinburg	1	3	0
Total	17	56	5
2006			
Moscow	5	11	1
Moscow region	3	7	0
St. Petersburg	3	10	4
Altayskiy territory	1	1	1
Belgorod	1	11	1
Birobigan	1	3	
Kaluga Region	1	2	0
Kostroma	2	7	5
Nizhniy Novgorod	4	6	Unknown
Novosibirsk	1	Unknown	Unknown
Oryol	2	6^4	2^4
Rostov on Don	1	2	0
Saratov	1	5	0
Tomsk	1	3	0
Ufa	1	3	3
Voronezh	1	13	7
Yekaterinburg	3	8^5	0
Yuzhno-Sakhalin.	1	1	0
Total	33	109^6	24^7

---

4   Estimated minimum; in one case, it is only known that a sentence has been passed.
5   Incl. 3 convicted for setting up an extremist community and for a murder where the hate motive was not recognized.

	NUMBER OF CONVICTIONS	*NUMBER OF OFFENDERS CONVICTED*	*INCLUDING CONDITIONAL SENTENCES OR RELEASE FROM PUNISHMENT*
2007			
Moscow	5	13	0
St. Petersburg	2	11	3
Belgorod	1	2	0
Kaluga	1	3	2
Krasnoyarsk	1	2	1
Leningrad Region	1	1	0
Nalchik	1	1	0
Nizhniy Novgorod	1	9	9
Omsk	1	1	0
Stavropol	2	2	0
Syktyvkar	1	1	0
Tambov	1	1	0
Tumen	1	6	2
Voronezh	1	4	0
Yaroslavl	1	1	1
Yekaterinburg	3	9	0
Total	24	67	18

---

6   Estimated minimum.
7   Estimated minimum.

Table 7: Statistics of convictions for hate propaganda in 2004-2007

CITY	NUMBER OF CONVICTIONS	NUMBER OF OFFENDERS CONVICTED	INCLUDING CONDITIONAL SENTENCES OR RELEASE FROM PUNISHMENT
2004			
Izhevsk	1	1	1
Novgorod	1	1	0
Novosibirsk	1	1	1
Total	3	3	2
2005			
Moscow	1	1	1
Khabarovsk	1	1	0
Kemerovo Region	4	4[1]	1
Kirov	1	1	0
Nalchik	1	1	1
Novgorod	1	3	0
Oryol	1	2	2
Syktyvkar	1	1	1
Yekaterinburg	1	1	0
Total	12	15	6
2006			
Moscow	1	1	0
Moscow region	1	1	0
St. Petersburg	2	2	1
Astrakhan region	1	1	0
Chelyabinsk	1	3	0
Kemerovo	2	2	2
Kirov	1	1	0
Krasnodar	1	1	0
Novgorod	1	1	0

---

1   One individual was convicted twice within one year; he faced the same charges, but
    for different incidents.

Samara	2	2	2
Saratov	1	1	1
Syktyvkar	1	1	0
Yekaterinburg	1	1	0
Yaroslavl	1	2	1
Total	17	20	7

2007			
Moscow	1	1	1
Barnaul	1	1	1
Blagoveschensk	1	1	0
Chelyabinsk	1	1	0
Kaliningrad	1	1	1
Kaluga	1	8	0
Kirov	1	1	0
Krasnodar	3	3	2
Kurgan	1	1	0
Maykop	1	1	0
Novgorod	1	1	0
Novosibirsk	3	3	0
Ryazan	1	2	0
Samara	1	2	2
Stavropol	1	1	1
Syktyvkar	3	3^2	0
Ulyanovsk	1	1	1
Vladimir	1	1	0
Vologda region	1	1	1
Yakutia	1	2	0
Yekaterinburg	1	1	0
Total	27	37	10

2　One individual was convicted twice within one year; he faced the same charges, but for different incidents.

Afterword

I am pleased to take this opportunity to share a few of my thoughts with the reader. First, a substantial part of this valuable book is devoted to a statistical analysis of hate crimes in Russia. This analysis reveals important trends and patterns of such crimes. However, the absolute numbers are meaningful only within the context of the society in which they were gathered. The following story illustrates this point.

When California Deputy Attorney General Kathleen W. Mikkelson wrote her review[1] of V. Likhachev's earlier book on antisemitism in Russia,[2] she tried to put Likhachev's data in perspective, but instead, came up with this paradox. In California, with a population of approximately 36 million people, 157 antisemitic hate crimes were reported in 2005. According to Likhachev's findings, 18 major attacks on Jews and Jewish property were reported in Russia, with a population of 146 million, in 2000. Therefore, if we calculate the incidence of the antisemitic crimes per thousand people, California's incidence would be 36 times higher than Russia's.

That ridiculous conclusion is a result of two faulty assumptions. First, the two societies have different thresholds of what constitutes antisemitism. Second, the vast majority of such hate crimes, like threatening messages or physical assaults, go unreported in Russia, where an act of reporting itself is a sign of assertiveness. Eventually, K. Mikkelson realized that the comparison was meaningless and deleted that part from her review. Analogously, the reported hate crimes against gays in California undoubtedly outnumber hate crimes against gays in Iran and Saudi Arabia. In fact, I suspect that no hate crimes are reported against gays in Iran or Saudi Arabia at all, as homosexuality is a crime punishable by death there.

Speaking of homophobia, it is not covered in the book as thoroughly as other phobias, probably because fighting homophobia in Russia is still an up-

---

1   K. Mikkelson, Book Review, *Demokratizatsiya*, Vol. 15, No. 2, 2007, pp. 268-272.
2   V. Likhachev, *Political Anti-Semitism in Post-Soviet Russia* (Stuttgart: *ibidem*-Verlag 2006).

hill battle. Even though homosexuality was decriminalized in Russia in 1993, the prevailing attitude of the Russian society toward gays is much more hostile than it is in the United States or Western Europe.

My next point is concerned with the future. After the book was written, President Vladimir Putin announced his choice for his successor, Dmitri Medvedev, a 42-year-old lawyer who served as Putin's chief of staff. Given Putin's popularity, it is likely that Medvedev will become the next Russian president. The manner in which he was chosen notwithstanding, the human rights community hailed that choice, or at least expressed cautious optimism. On several occasions, Medvedev has taken a strong stand against Russian hate groups, which earned him an endorsement from the Russian Orthodox Patriarch, Alexy II, the Chief Rabbi of Russia, Berl Lazar, and the Council of Mufties of Russia.

As of this writing, the presidential election in Russia is still two months away. Even if Medvedev is elected, it remains to be seen how he and Putin will share power. (On the next day after his nomination, Medvedev returned the favor by nominating Putin to become his Prime Minister.) Nevertheless, Medvedev's nomination seems to be good news for human rights in Russia.

Finally, I would like to clarify an issue that belongs to the realm of linguistics, but that sometimes spills over to the political arena. There are three commonly used spellings of the same word in English: anti-Semitism, anti-semitism and antisemitism. I consistently used the last one in this book and my rationale is based in part on Walter Laqueur's historical arguments[3]. The word "antisemitism" was a neologism popularized by a German journalist named W. Marr in 1879. He published an anti-Jewish pamphlet attacking the Jews from a non-religious point of view.

Since then, the term antisemitism and its adjective form – antisemitic – have meant exactly that, "anti-Jewish". Despite its appearance, the term has nothing to do with a broader meaning – "against all Semitic peoples": Arabs, Jews, Phoenicians, Canaanites, etc. Obviously, antisemites have nothing against Hannibal, who was a Carthaginian (the Carthaginians were a people of Phoenician descent).

---

3   W. Laqueur, *The Changing Face of Antisemitism* (New York: Oxford University Press 2006).

Yet, this semantic nuance has been abused in the propaganda area. Thus, a Saudi official, who was questioned on American television about antisemitism in Saudi Arabia, found an easy way out. He simply claimed that the Saudis could not possibly be antisemites, because, as Arabs, they belong to the Semitic group of peoples. The suggested spelling of this term as one word makes it clearer that it is a neologism with a meaning unrelated to its etymology. Finally, let me quote Bernard Lewis:[4] "Antisemitism has never anywhere been concerned with anyone but Jews."

Eugene Veklerov
Albany, California
January 2008

---

4   B. Lewis, *Semites and Antisemites* (London: The Library Press 1973).

SOVIET AND POST-SOVIET POLITICS AND SOCIETY

Edited by Dr. Andreas Umland

ISSN 1614-3515

14   *Nathan D. Larson*
Alexander Solzhenitsyn and the
Russo-Jewish Question
ISBN 3-89821-483-4

15   *Guido Houben*
Kulturpolitik und Ethnizität
Staatliche Kunstförderung im Russland der
neunziger Jahre
Mit einem Vorwort von Gert Weisskirchen
ISBN 3-89821-542-3

16   *Leonid Luks*
Der russische „Sonderweg"?
Aufsätze zur neuesten Geschichte Russlands
im europäischen Kontext
ISBN 3-89821-496-6

17   *Евгений Мороз*
История «Мёртвой воды» – от
страшной сказки к большой
политике
Политическое неоязычество в
постсоветской России
ISBN 3-89821-551-2

18   *Александр Верховский и Галина
Кожевникова (ред.)*
Этническая и религиозная
интолерантность в российских СМИ
Результаты мониторинга 2001-2004 гг.
ISBN 3-89821-569-5

19   *Christian Ganzer*
Sowjetisches Erbe und ukrainische
Nation
Das Museum der Geschichte des Zaporoger
Kosakentums auf der Insel Chortycja
Mit einem Vorwort von Frank Golczewski
ISBN 3-89821-504-0

20   *Эльза-Баир Гучинова*
Помнить нельзя забыть
Антропология депортационной травмы
калмыков
С предисловием Кэролайн Хамфри
ISBN 3-89821-506-7

21   *Юлия Лидерман*
Мотивы «проверки» и «испытания»
в постсоветской культуре
Советское прошлое в российском
кинематографе 1990-х годов
С предисловием Евгения Марголита
ISBN 3-89821-511-3

22   *Tanya Lokshina, Ray Thomas, Mary
Mayer (Eds.)*
The Imposition of a Fake Political
Settlement in the Northern Caucasus
The 2003 Chechen Presidential Election
ISBN 3-89821-436-2

23   *Timothy McCajor Hall, Rosie Read
(Eds.)*
Changes in the Heart of Europe
Recent Ethnographies of Czechs, Slovaks,
Roma, and Sorbs
With an afterword by Zdeněk Salzmann
ISBN 3-89821-606-3

24   *Christian Autengruber*
Die politischen Parteien in Bulgarien
und Rumänien
Eine vergleichende Analyse seit Beginn der
90er Jahre
Mit einem Vorwort von Dorothée de Nève
ISBN 3-89821-476-1

25   *Annette Freyberg-Inan with Radu
Cristescu*
The Ghosts in Our Classrooms, or:
John Dewey Meets Ceauşescu
The Promise and the Failures of Civic
Education in Romania
ISBN 3-89821-416-8

26   *John B. Dunlop*
The 2002 Dubrovka and 2004 Beslan
Hostage Crises
A Critique of Russian Counter-Terrorism
With a foreword by Donald N. Jensen
ISBN 3-89821-608-X

27   *Peter Koller*
Das touristische Potenzial von
Kam''janec'–Podil's'kyj
Eine fremdenverkehrsgeographische
Untersuchung der Zukunftsperspektiven und
Maßnahmenplanung zur
Destinationsentwicklung des „ukrainischen
Rothenburg"
Mit einem Vorwort von Kristiane Klemm
ISBN 3-89821-640-3

28   *Françoise Daucé, Elisabeth Sieca-
Kozlowski (Eds.)*
Dedovshchina in the Post-Soviet
Military
Hazing of Russian Army Conscripts in a
Comparative Perspective
With a foreword by Dale Herspring
ISBN 3-89821-616-0

75   Heiko Pleines (Hrsg.)
     Corporate Governance in post-
     sozialistischen Volkswirtschaften
     ISBN 978-3-89821-766-8

76   Stefan Ihrig
     Wer sind die Moldawier?
     Rumänismus versus Moldowanismus in
     Historiographie und Schulbüchern der
     Republik Moldova, 1991-2006
     Mit einem Vorwort von Holm Sundhaussen
     ISBN 978-3-89821-466-7

77   Galina Kozhevnikova in collaboration
     with Alexander Verkhovsky and
     Eugene Veklerov
     Ultra-Nationalism and Hate Crimes in
     Contemporary Russia
     The 2004-2006 Annual Reports of Moscow's
     SOVA Center
     With a foreword by Stephen D. Shenfield
     ISBN 978-3-89821-868-9

78   Florian Küchler
     The Role of the European Union in
     Moldova's Transnistria Conflict
     With a foreword by Christopher Hill
     ISBN 978-3-89821-850-4

FORTHCOMING (MANUSCRIPT
WORKING TITLES)

Stephanie Solowyda
Biography of Semen Frank
ISBN 3-89821-457-5

Margaret Dikovitskaya
Arguing with the Photographs
Russian Imperial Colonial Attitudes in Visual Culture
ISBN 3-89821-462-1

Sergei M. Plekhanov
Russian Nationalism in the Age of
Globalization
ISBN 3-89821-484-2

Robert Pyrah
Cultural Memory and Identity
Literature, Criticism and the Theatre in Lviv - Lwow -
Lemberg, 1918-1939 and in post-Soviet Ukraine
ISBN 3-89821-505-9

Andrei Rogatchevski
The National-Bolshevik Party
ISBN 3-89821-532-6

Zenon Victor Wasyliw
Soviet Culture in the Ukrainian Village
The Transformation of Everyday Life and Values,
1921-1928
ISBN 3-89821-536-9

Nele Sass
Das gegenkulturelle Milieu im
postsowjetischen Russland
ISBN 3-89821-543-1

Julie Elkner
Maternalism versus Militarism
The Russian Soldiers' Mothers Committee
ISBN 3-89821-575-X

Alexandra Kamarowsky
Russia's Post-crisis Growth
ISBN 3-89821-580-6

Martin Friessnegg
Das Problem der Medienfreiheit in Russland
seit dem Ende der Sowjetunion
ISBN 3-89821-588-1

Nikolaj Nikiforowitsch Borobow
Führende Persönlichkeiten in Russland vom
12. bis 20 Jhd.: Ein Lexikon
Aus dem Russischen übersetzt und herausgegeben von
Eberhard Schneider
ISBN 3-89821-638-1

Martin Malek, Anna Schor-Tschudnowskaja
Tschetschenien und die Gleichgültigkeit
Europas
Russlands Kriege und die Agonie der Idee der
Menschenrechte
ISBN 3-89821-676-4

Andreas Langenohl
Political Culture and Criticism of Society
Intellectual Articulations in Post-Soviet Russia
ISBN 3-89821-709-4

Thomas Borén
Meeting Places in Transformation
ISBN 3-89821-739-6

Lars Löckner
Sowjetrussland in der Beurteilung der
Emigrantenzeitung 'Rul', 1920-1924
ISBN 3-89821-741-8

Ekaterina Taratuta
The Red Line of Construction
Semantics and Mythology of a Siberian Heliopolis
ISBN 3-89821-742-6

Bernd Kappenberg
Zeichen setzen für Europa
Der Gebrauch europäischer lateinischer Sonderzeichen
in der deutschen Öffentlichkeit
ISBN 3-89821-749-3

Siegbert Klee, Martin Sandhop, Oxana
Schwajka, Andreas Umland
Elitenbildung in der Postsowjetischen
Ukraine
ISBN 978-389821-829-0

Natalya Ketenci
The effect of location on the performance of
Kazakhstani industrial enterprises in the
transition period
ISBN 978-389821-831-3

Quotes from reviews of SPPS volumes:

On vol. 1 – *The Implementation of the ECHR in Russia*: "Full of examples, experiences and valuable observations which could provide the basis for new strategies."
Diana Schmidt, *Неприкосновенный запас*, 2005

On vol. 2 – *Putins Russland*: "Wipperfürth draws attention to little known facts. For instance, the Russians have still more positive feelings towards Germany than to any other non-Slavic country."
Oldag Kaspar, *Süddeutsche Zeitung*, 2005

On vol. 3 – *Die Übernahme internationalen Rechts in die russische Rechtsordnung*: "Hussner's is an interesting, detailed and, at the same time, focused study which deals with all relevant aspects and contains insights into contemporary Russian legal thought."
Herbert Küpper, *Jahrbuch für Ostrecht*, 2005

On vol. 5 – *Квадратные метры, определяющие сознание*: „Meerovich provides a study that will be of considerable value to housing specialists and policy analysts."
Christina Varga-Harris, *Slavic Review*, 2006

On vol. 6 – *New Directions in Russian International Studies*: "A helpful step in the direction of an overdue dialogue between Western and Russian IR scholarly communities."
Diana Schmidt, *Europe-Asia Studies*, 2006

On vol. 8 – *Nation-Building and Minority Politics in Post-Socialist States:* "Galbreath's book is an admirable and craftsmanlike piece of work, and should be read by all specialists interested in the Baltic area."
Andrejs Plakans, *Slavic Review*, 2007

On vol. 9 – *Народы Кавказа в Вооружённых силах СССР:* "In this superb new book, Bezugolnyi skillfully fashions an accurate and candid record of how and why the Soviet Union mobilized and employed the various ethnic groups in the Caucasus region in the Red Army's World War II effort."
David J. Glantz, *Journal of Slavic Military Studies*, 2006

On vol. 10 – *Русское Национальное Единство*: "Pribylovskii's and Likhachev's work is likely to remain the definitive study of the Russian National Unity for a very long time."
Mischa Gabowitsch, *e-Extreme*, 2006

On vol. 13 – *The Politicization of Russian Orthodoxy*: "Mitrofanova's book is a fascinating study which raises important questions about the type of national ideology that will come to predominate in the new Russia."
Zoe Knox, *Europe-Asia Studies*, 2006

On vol. 14 – *Aleksandr Solzhenitsyn and the Modern Russo-Jewish Question*: "Larson has written a well-balanced survey of Solzhenitsyn's writings on Russian-Jewish relations."

Nikolai Butkevich, *e-Extreme*, 2006

On vol. 16 – *Der russische Sonderweg?:* "Luks's remarkable knowledge of the history of this wide territory from the Elbe to the Pacific Ocean and his life experience give his observations a particular sharpness and his judgements an exceptional weight."

Peter Krupnikow, *Mitteilungen aus dem baltischen Leben*, 2006

On vol. 17 – *История «Мёртвой воды»*: "Moroz provides one of the best available surveys of Russian neo-paganism."

Mischa Gabowitsch, *e-Extreme*, 2006

On vol. 18 – *Этническая и религиозная интолерантность в российских СМИ:* "A constructive contribution to a crucial debate about media-endorsed intolerance which has once again flared up in Russia."

Mischa Gabowitsch, *e-Extreme*, 2006

On vol. 25 – *The Ghosts in Our Classroom*: "Freyberg-Inan's well-researched and incisive monograph, balanced and informed about Romanian education in general, should be required reading for those Eurocrats who have shaped Romanian spending priorities since 2000."

Tom Gallagher, *Slavic Review*, 2006

On vol. 26 – *The 2002 Dubrovka and 2004 Beslan Hostage Crises:* "Dunlop's analysis will help to draw Western attention to the plight of those who have suffered by these terrorist acts, and the importance, for all Russians, of uncovering the truth of about what happened."

Amy Knight, *Times Literary Supplement*, 2006

On vol. 29 – *Zivilgesellschaftliche Einflüsse auf die Orange Revolution*: „Strasser's study constitutes an outstanding empirical analysis and well-grounded location of the subject within theory."

Heiko Pleines, *Osteuropa*, 2006

On vol. 34 – *Postsowjetische Feiern*: "Mühlfried's book contains not only a solid ethnographic study, but also points at some problems emerging from Georgia's prevalent understanding of culture."

Godula Kosack, *Anthropos*, 2007

On vol. 35 – *Fascism Past and Present, West and East*: "Committed students will find much of interest in these sometimes barbed exchanges."

Robert Paxton, *Journal of Global History*, 2007

Series Subscription

Please enter my subscription to the series *Soviet and Post-Soviet Politics and Society*, ISSN 1614-3515, as follows:

❏ complete series   OR   ❏ English-language titles
                                       ❏ German-language titles
                                       ❏ Russian-language titles
starting with
❏ volume # 1
❏ volume # ___
    ❏ please also include the following volumes: #___, ___, ___, ___, ___, ___, ___
❏ the next volume being published
    ❏ please also include the following volumes: #___, ___, ___, ___, ___, ___, ___

❏ 1 copy per volume   OR   ❏ ___ copies per volume

Subscription within Germany:
You will receive every volume at 1st publication at the regular bookseller's price – incl. s & h and VAT.
Payment:
❏ Please bill me for every volume.
❏ Lastschriftverfahren: Ich/wir ermächtige(n) Sie hiermit widerruflich, den Rechnungsbetrag je Band von meinem/unserem folgendem Konto einzuziehen.

Kontoinhaber: _____Kreditinstitut: _____

Kontonummer: _____Bankleitzahl:_____

International Subscription:
Payment (incl. s & h and VAT) in advance for
❏ 10 volumes/copies (€ 319.80)   ❏ 20 volumes/copies (€ 599.80)
❏ 40 volumes/copies (€ 1,099.80)
Please send my books to:

NAME_____DEPARTMENT_____
ADDRESS _____
POST/ZIP CODE_____COUNTRY _____
TELEPHONE _____EMAIL_____

date/signature_____

A hint for librarians in the former Soviet Union: Your academic library might be eligible to receive free-of-cost scholarly literature from Germany via the German Research Foundation. For Russian-language information on this program, see
    http://www.dfg.de/forschungsfoerderung/formulare/download/12_54.pdf.

Please fax to: **0511 / 262 2201 (+49 511 262 2201)**
or mail to: *ibidem*-Verlag, Julius-Leber-Weg 11, D-30457 Hannover,Germany
or send an e-mail: ibidem@ibidem-verlag.de

ibidem-Verlag

Melchiorstr. 15

D-70439 Stuttgart

info@ibidem-verlag.de

www.ibidem-verlag.de
www.edition-noema.de
www.autorenbetreuung.de

www.ingramcontent.com/pod-product-compliance
Lightning Source LLC
Chambersburg PA
CBHW050713280326
41926CB00088B/3015